THE BOOK OF
BAMPTON

CAROLINE SEWARD

HALSGROVE

First published in Great Britain in 1998
Reprinted 2003

British Library Cataloguing-in-Publication Data
A CIP record for this title is available from the British Library

ISBN 1 85522 646 4

HALSGROVE
Halsgrove House
Lower Moor Way
Tiverton, Devon EX16 6SS
T: 01884 243242
F: 01884 243325
www.halsgrove.com

DEDICATION

To Reg Kingdon
and to the people of Bampton

Printed and bound in Great Britain by CPI Bath Press, Bath

Contents

Acknowledgements

I have many kind people to thank with great sincerity as they have either lent files, treasured photographs, whole scrapbooks, or filled me in with all sorts of detail necessary to complete this book. Reg and Joyce Kingdon must take priority. A big thank you to Reg who was so delighted to think his hobby has been acknowledged as a major part of the more recent history of Bampton. I have only used a broad selection so there is plenty left for a second edition, Reg! Joyce has been a tower of strength, as Jack and Florrie Gillard have been, reading and correcting any parts of the story needing adjustment. Their encouragement has helped me enormously, thank you, my dear friends..We all know how much Reg would have loved to be able to write this book himself. We hope our efforts wiil please him!

Don Gould and Arnold Seward are the other two people capable of going well back into the present century, coupled with a keen knowledge of longer ago. Alas, Arnold will not see the book but I feel he probably has been watching my writing efforts, while Don Gould, despite his wife's illness, has been a great source of help to me, too.

Sally Luxton, Eileen Shere, Mrs Currie, Julie Watson and Bampton Women's Institute have kindly lent treasured collections in scrapbooks and albums. You will see some of your pictures and information scattered through the book. Thank you all. Julie has added a unique slant to *The Book of Bampton* with her humourous memories of local folk. Thank you so much Julie for allowing us to use your talent.

Big thanks must go to my husband, Brian, who has been a competent cameraman wherever needed, while the rest of the family, Roger and Dawn, and our willing staff have made sure that I had as much time out of our shop as I needed to produce this book.

Thanks to Revd Tony Grosse and Bill Bampton for archive material; Bill Hancock too for loaning his archive collection. Thanks also to my grandsons, Anthony and Patrick, who I missed out on babysitting during the writing of the book!

Special thanks to Dorrie Seward, Dorothy Ellicott, Alan and Anne Collard and Geoff Chamberlain, Rex Serenger, Michael Rendell, Dr Tony Baker, Revd Paul Ockford, Judith Coney, Margaret Hellier, Alan Rowland, Nicky Hayes, Ray and Phyll Marley, Alan Dixson, John Record, Joy Coles, Anne Bennett, Alec and Joan Attwater, Aubrey Besley, Brian Smith, Kathleen Burnett, Bridgette Burnett, Christopher Burnett, Danny Penny, June Coles, Lilian Edworthy, Margaret and Derek Aldridge, Diana Thomas, Sylvia Jansen, Rosemary Woodward, and Wendy Marchment. I have enjoyed our chats and greatly appreciate your contributions.

Thanks also to Margaret Baker, Janet Holloway, the *Mid Devon Gazette*, Dick Sloman, Stuart Bennett, Ray and Isabelle Kenny, Herbie Cleverley and Clifford Lazarus. Also the Ven. Tony Tremlett.

It is impossible to mention everyone who has helped, as there have been so many. Even to those not listed - a big thank you. One last person must be mentioned, Denise Lyons. It was Denise who suggested that I should put this book together for Reg. I have enjoyed the challenge, thank you Denise.

The photographs are credited individually, RK denotes the Reg Kingdon Collection, BS Brian Seward. Every effort has been made to correctly identify the owner of other images - apologies to anyone who may have been inadvertently missed.

FOREWORD

Bampton has many things in its favour. First is the central position it holds between Exeter and Minehead, Taunton and Barnstaple - the crossroads of old trading routes. For today's commuters, shoppers, or for leisure, each of these places takes roughly half an hour to reach by car.

Bampton lies in a bowl between soft green fields and lots of wonderful woods full of gnarled old trees, offering protection and habitat for the abundant wildlife; ideal conditions for wild flowers and fauna. Our castle mound makes a pleasant view point over this countryside, while picturing it as a fortress is more difficult. Stand on top of any hill overlooking Bampton and your eye will immediately be drawn to the bell tower of St Michael and All Angels, the lovely Parish Church built from local stone. The quarry behind the Exeter Inn was in use about the time it is thought the present St Michaels was built. The sound of the six bells in full peal drifting up to meet you in your lofty view point is unforgettable. To think that Alan Collard actually climbed up the flag pole on top of the tower says something about the innocent bravado of yesteryear. And he was caught by the Rev Frayling!

Look down from the church tower and Bampton lies all around the church in a tidy pattern, with the Shutter Brook and River Batherm running in sort of T-formation through the centre of the town. The town has a similar population to the olden days, the difference today is that there are fewer large families sharing homes, so the number of houses has increased.

As one part of history ends a new part begins in the same spot, such as the railway station west of the church, now deeply buried beneath a car park and children's playground, while a small, modern industrial estate sits where the railway sidings used to be in constant use. Modern life requires these facilities but nostalgia surrounds the demise of the Puffing Billies that first allowed folk the opportunity to explore the surrounding area, while providing transport of livestock, prior to motor vehicles. Travelling the Exe Valley by train was really special.

For leisure Bampton is only a couple of miles from the south-east corner of the exquisite Exmoor National Park. Within ten minutes you can be walking on moorland whilst enjoying the peacefulness of Wimbleball Lake and marvel at the fine array of colours that continually change with the weather and time of day, and possibly glimpse the wild red deer. A few miles further and the forest of Exmoor is yours in all its glory. But do not expect to see a forest of trees!

Our story is about much more than boundaries and buildings. Without the people of Bampton we have no story. It is about the way they have lived and used those old buildings, the progression of Bampton Fair, the introduction and later demise of the railway, the quarrying industry and it's closure, and how the mechanised world has replaced the loyal bonds between man and horse.

I am in no way a historian but I was delighted to have the chance to present this book, to highlight one man's dedication to a village that I love, and the fascinating life that makes up this pictorial memory. I prefer to call Bampton a village, as many others do, because I feel for its size it can in no way be a town. Our success in the Britain in Bloom competition as a large village supports this view. Also, Bampton has a warm and friendly atmosphere far better related to a village and, although as a market town, the markets disappeared long ago, I will refer through the text to Bampton as a town.

'How do you want the book written?' I asked.

'Well you said Reg Kingdon has a great collection of Old Bampton, so start there!' was the publisher's reply. Each one of these Parish History books are bound to be different, as each village has special individual secrets pertaining to it's past, all waiting to be recorded lest they be forgotten. Of course I began by chatting to Reg and Joyce Kingdon. Then we decided to throw open an invitation to anyone in the Parish who had a story to tell through spoken memories or photographs. I could easily have confined the story to Reg's wonderful and fascinating collection, but I am glad that our invitation made people turn out drawers and cupboards, under the stairs, up in their lofts, as I have been inundated with all kinds of memorabilia that could only enhance Reg's collection.

Other people have lent me treasured scrapbooks with all kinds of things in them. I felt very honoured to be allowed to use their material. I have thoroughly enjoyed talking to many local people and I am indebted for their kind co-operation. I only hope I have done justice to their time and help.

Much of this book is made up from photograph taken over the past hundred years or so. While compiling it the one thought that struck me is that how I wish we had photographs of the years before then, they could have filled volumes! Take a good look at all those faces in the earliest pictures and ask yourself how interesting it would be to learn about their families and predecessors. How did they really cope with the hard life we know they endured? What did Bampton Castle really look like when it was fortified and lived in? Who was that happy-looking elderly gentleman in the 1890 chuchyard photograph? Who were his family? Where did he live?

Sally Luxton has a scrapbook that made me smile when I opened it. There I found a story I had written for our two sons thirty years ago, called *The Little Red Tractor*. It was published in the *West Somerset Free Press*. Since that time another author has made themselves famous with a series of the same nature! A missed opportunity!

Two other people have been great sources of help in producing this book. The first is Donald Gould who lived in Bampton and worked at Scotts Quarries. He saw the Scott family develop the quarry workings from the days of horses up to the present day, growing from a local name to one whose fame as a reliable workforce brought work from far and wide. The other person was my father-in-law, Arnold Seward. He fascinated me with tales of his life through the bakery of long ago and eventually took up my challenge and wrote his memories down in an exercise book, as and when they came to him. Sometimes they were only written on scraps of paper, but vivid and real to read.

All three men Reg, Donald and Arnold show how deeply proud they feel to be Bamptonians, and it is this depth of feelings that has been my task to convey to you, the reader. At first when I sat down alone in the bedroom with all these boxes of files and treasures I had my doubts whether I could write the book as Reg, Don and Arnold would wish to read it. Once I opened up the first few files and people began showing an interest by bringing in their contributions it fell into sections, quite easily. I wanted to cover as much ground as possible to show how everyday life was for the ordinary person who lived and worked in Bampton.

Talking to our older residents there is one word that links them all - pride. Yes, pride for the kind of life they grew up in and worked through. Their lives were harder, without frills, especially out on the farms, but in their simplicity was a great pride in all they owned and worked to maintain. Urban life is becoming harder and more pressurised, as we know by the constant stream of people wanting to move down here. Has progress made our generation contented and proud? How will our generation's story read in a hundred years' time?

With all the changes of today I want Bampton to always be remembered as the happy, friendly and beautiful village I have lived in for forty years.

Caroline Seward
Bampton 1998

INTRODUCTION

by Brian Seward

When this book was being planned it was never intended to be an academic history book. The principal idea was to let people see a portrait of Bampton since the earliest photographs were produced. During that period of 100 to 150 years ago, technology has gradually become a factor in everyone's life and progress has been rapid and far-reaching in a relatively short period of time. Before that time the lives of people in Bampton revolved around agriculture and rural pursuits, remaining largely unchanged over the centuries. In the seventeenth and eighteenth centuries it grew in importance as a market town known for its sheep fairs, and it's name was celebrated in a breed of sheep known as Bampton Notts. The woollen trade started to decline towards the end of the eighteenth century.

A number of people have kindly given the author details of the Bampton Hundred (an early administrative division of the county structure with its own court), and information from the archives has helped to bring about this story of Bampton, known in the tenth century as Badentone, and later as Baunton. So we are a part of Devon and, yes, we had our own court until about 1913.

The Bampton Hundred comprises seven parishes: Bampton, Clayhanger, Hockworthy, Holcombe Rogus, Morebath, Uffculm and Burlescombe. The area has long been noted for its limestone quarries and its sheep, and some early references are made to a 'chalybeate spring', water rich in iron and mineral salts, but where it was sited, is not clear.

The Lordship of the Manor went with the ownership of Coombehead, which is sited one mile to the north-west of the town, on the road towards Dulverton.

In early times it is probable that our Celtic ancestors first lived around a ford in the river in the area now known as Briton Street. During the middle of the first century the Romans arrived and fortified an area with a mound and ditches to subdue the locals. Roman coins and artifacts have been found locally. With the onset of the fall of the Roman Empire in the fourth century, their dominance waned and this left a vacuum to be filled by the Saxons. They increased the settlement with a New Tun, or town, sited around what is now Newton Square. The Manor was with the Manor of Molland, and was the property of the Saxon king.

The Domesday Book records Bampton with 31 Villagers, 20 Smallholders, 15 Pigmen, 2 Slaves and an unrecorded number of women and children. In 1066 the Normans paid their famous visit to Hastings. William the Conqueror distributed the spoils to his cronies, and the Barony of Bathermton (Bampton) was given to Walter de Douai, known as 'The Fleming', being Flemish. It appears he was probably William's castle-building engineer in these parts. He increased the fortification of the earlier castle, and the mound (Motte) he built is still visible. Around this a Bailey, or semi-protected area, gave shelter to the Baron's army, tradesmen and animals.

The only military action known to have taken place was the siege of 1136, when Walter s son, Robert, who was accused by his adversary, the Bishop of Bath, to be a small-time drunken tyrant, attempted to bluff King Stephen in a dispute over Church lands. Robert realised he was in hot water and when he met the king he appeared to be deeply penitent. The king sent him off under armed escort, but when the soldiers arrived at one of his mansions, Robert wined and dined them lavishly and while they slept it off he disappeared.

The king sought retribution and laid seige to Robert's supporters, under his son Robert junior, in Bampton Castle. On seeing one of their number captured and hanged the castle was surrendered and Robert's son fled to the protection of King David of Scotland. Robert senior may have sought safety with Baldwin De Redvers who was holding Exeter against the king at Rougemont Castle. He later fled to David and may later have been killed at the Battle of the Standard in Yorkshire. He is stated to have died 'a miserable death amongst strangers'.

The Barony passed to the Paganell Family and then to the Cogans. In 1336 Richard Cogan was issued a royal licence to fortify his mansion. This is not proven to be on the Motte and Bailey site, although evidence of a large amount of building stone has been found on the Motte recently by archeologists.

The Castle was last occupied in the early 1500s, probably a short time before the Bourchier Family became Lords of the Manor. It is believed that the remains of William and Sir John Bourchier, Earl of Bath are buried in the Parish Church.

LORD OF THE MANOR

Geoffrey White, whose family once owned Coombehead and the Lordship of the Manor, wrote the following for this book:

Coombehead was bought in 1895 by William White, my Grandfather, along with Coldharbour, Rows and Benshayes Farms and the Lordship of the Manor of Bampton. The Lordship covers Bampton, Stallenge Thorn, Highleigh and Duvale.

Previously William White had been in South Africa, having gone there for his health. He worked mainly at Kimberley and at one time was a junior secretary for Cecil Rhodes. He started the first Building Society in South Africa and was Captain of the Kimberley Cricket Club, which included his three brothers. He later founded Bampton Cricket Club.

William married Maud Elsworthy Hancock, one of many sisters who lived at Stag Mill, Uplowman. Her niece Anne Bennett lives in Bampton today. They had two sons, Rhodes and Leonard.

William White died in 1948, aged 94, and Coldharbour was sold to help with death duties, to the tenant, Eddy Mantle. William is buried in Bampton Churchyard, beside Leonard White. William's widow died in 1960, aged 88.

Looking east from the church tower, a view over the town to Bampton Castle. Author

Below: *The Castle mound looking north. The flat area on top of the mound was once fortified, probably with a wall of wooden stakes.* BS

Combehead, former home of William White, Lord of the Manor of Bampton. RK

Coombehead was sold again for death duties to Mr A.P. Baxter (Sandy). He had been a great cricketer, playing for Lancashire and Middlesex. He once bowled Don Bradman for a duck!

It was thought by Leonard and Rhodes that the Lordship of the Manor should go with the house, therefore both were sold together. On Mr Baxter's death his widow, having gone to live in Kent, thought the title should be given back to the Whites. It was given to Richard Hocken White, Grandson of Leonard. Richard lives at Minehead, being assistant racehorse trainer to Philip J. Hobbs, of Carhampton. Richard is an amateur jockey and rides both for his mother, Tessa, who trains several point-to-pointers at the family farm of Benshayes. Richard rides at point-to-point and National Hunt meetings. He has two brothers, Charlie and Rupert.

Benshayes Farm was recently used as the location for the film Land Girls.

A BAMPTON MURDER MSYTERY

When Bill Hampton was browsing throught the records of the fourteenth century, The Calendar of the Rolls of Edward II, he noted an interesting series of events pertaining to Bampton's past:

A writ was issued on 20 February 1315 for an Inquisition (or hearing) into the death of Thomas de Cogan, a Tenent in Chief, that is one who holds his land directly from the King. It states that he held land in Baunton (Bampton), Uffculm, Peterspenny, Nutsilver and Midsilver, together with Huntspill in Somerset, from the King, at one Knights fee. In other words he had, on request, to provide a knight to serve the king. In the Devon

records it is said that his son and heir, Richard, was aged sixteen at the time of his father's death. On that same day, Walter, the Bishop of Exeter, obtained Wardship of Richard. In April the Bishop obtained part of Richard's land, including Bampton for Wardship, paying the vast sum of £400.

Of course wheels turned slowly in the fourteenth century, but someone must have begun to 'smell a rat' over the death of Thomas de Cogan. The circuit Judges were brought in some months later and a commission followed. The Calendar Rolls state that on 2 November 1315 a Commission of 'Oyer et Terminer' (hear and determine) should be held by high ranking civil judges, Robert de Stockley and Mathew de Furness. To enquire into 'touching the persons who lately maliciously intoxicated Thomas de Cogan at Baunton, Devon.' In this context 'intoxicate' means to poison.

Although the outcome of the investigation remains unknown, we do know that on 10 April 1315 John Waiwayn, Escheator (one who distributes on behalf of the king), delivered to Petronella, wife of the late Thomas de Cogan, one third of Huntspill, one third of Uffculm and one third of Baunton. Later on 22 September 1315, Petronella was licensed, at a fee of £20, to marry 'whomsoever she will in the King's Fealty'. So here we leave the wealthy widow of the (murdered?) Baron of Bampton preparing to accept one of many suitors which she no doubt had!

The medieval history of Bampton and its castle attracts members of various societies who re-enact the lives of people of earlier days. Here Sue and Dave Greenhalgh and friends wear costumes that are authentic in every detail. Dave is one of the country's leading experts on British hammered coins of the period. Photo Dave Greenhalgh

An old photograph taken from the top of Ball Hill Lane showing West Street before the School Close, West Street and Meadow View development. RK

Chapter 1 - A Stroll Around Bampton

We know that the early settlers lived around Briton Street at the south end of the town Two packhorse routes crossed in Bampton and the river Batherm was a ford, part of the north-to-south route. Two early photographs show important changes in Briton Street since those days. Beneath the road where a row of eye-catching flower troughs stand, south of the river, is the remains of an old cobbled road. The surface must have been hard on the poor horses' feet and extremely uncomfortable to anyone riding in a cart or trap. Where New Buildings now stand look at the row of thatched cottages. Take note of their height, because they once stood on that old road level.

On the opposite side of Briton Street, and nearer the top, take a look at more thatched cottages. Winslade House and garden replaced them. Winslade House was for many years the doctor's surgery, where medicines were dispensed, and it was the home of well known local GP, Tony Baker, until he retired.

Brook Street is the wide street where many of the local businesses are to be found. In earlier days, until 1859, the river was open and the Shuttern Brook flowed through Brook Street (known then as Duckpaddle), down from the north of the town, via Frog Street, until it met the Batherm on the west side of the bridge. The Batherm Bridge was rebuilt in 1827, costing £654.

An aerial view of Bampton taken before the development of Bouchier Close and Market Close, showing the old Morebath Hill. A. Dixon

Above: *Looking down Briton Street to Batherm Bridge and Brook Street, c.1910. The thatched house on the right, is now replaced by New Buildings. Look at the level of the road!* RK

Left: *Briton Street, c.1890. The thatched cottages on the left are where Winslade House now stands, and was the doctor's surgery for many years. Behind the boys, left foreground, is the old Police Station.* RK

Possibly the earlier name of Duckpaddle was due to the duck population, ancestors of our present-day feathered friends who entertain the children of today!

Bampton has been heavily flooded in the past and great efforts have been made to counteract the problem. The photographs show how once closed-in the Shuttern was, later opened up again to widen the river bed. The water can now be diverted up into the pavement gutters by a lever in the Shuttern Brook in Frog Street. The gutter water disappears down a culvert just short of the bridge near Chalfont, the house with a railed garden. In the summer the flowing gutters stay

This page and opposite - a panoramic view of the River Bridge from a painitng dated 1900. RK

Left: *Brook Street around 1900, looking north. The Post Office is today in the building with the dormer windows on the right, but it was previously in the shop on the left, and also in the premises which is today the fish and chip shop.* RK

Feeding ducks - an age-old delight for Bampton children. BS

Looking up Brook Street, c.1900. The vet's surgery was a house. Next up from Coren's was also a business by the look of the sign over the door.

clean and are a big help for watering the flower displays. If you stop and think about it, Brook Street is just a long river bridge.

The great width of Brook Street has been captured on many historic photographs, showing exactly how industrious Bampton has always been. The width and length of the street is ideal for the many marches, parades and street parties, let alone the famous Fair Day held here. In these present times, when vehicles outnumber private garages, Bampton must be thankful that the width of Brook street enables out-of-town shoppers to support the local traders with easy parking.

Elsewhere in Brook Street some of the present-day buildings show signs of renovation, but their original structure remains. Take Costcutters, for instance. This was a two-storey property until relatively recent times. The Blamey's built the top storey on Costcutters and they also built the Post Office. Jack Blamey's grandfather put pennies between the yellow bricks as the Post Office was being built.

The Blamey's came to Bampton to build the railway bridges and most of the ones still visible (and those that have gone) were built by them.

At the north end of Brook Street is a road junction. This has changed considerably over the years. At the east end of the island, where local councillor Rex Serenger has his hardware store and petrol pumps, there were once more houses. On the opposite side of the road you can sit and appreciate the stage floral displays, today, but at the expense of more houses and a business that were demolished to widen the road. During the war the American tanks used to regularly knock pieces off those properties as they tried to negoti-

Top: *Lower end of Brook Street, looking south. The quarry workings are in view; also note the position of the well at Well House (centre right).* RK

Middle: *Brook Street looking towards Batherm Bridge, c.1900.* RK

Right: *Looking south down Brook Street, c.1900. Two women stand outside G.F. Escott's shop carrying shopping, a delivery boy stands centre with a wicker basket on his shoulder, while the boy on the left is on crutches, perhaps a victim of polio.* RK

Above: *The top of Brook Street, looking into Fore Street and 'Staddons' c.1900.* RK

Castle Street c.1900. The building on the right was demolished and is now the 'Stage'. RK

Work on the culvert containing the Shuttern Brook after widening it in order to prevent flooding in Frog Street, Silver Street and Brook Street. The brook ran open in Brook Street until 1859 but the original culvert was too small to carry heavy rainwater.

ate the narrow bend. At one time this road was merely a cart track. Further on we come upon an old thatched building, this time stables, which later became the Serenger store. Mr Serenger's mother's father, Ross Butler, bought it and founded the family business.

Castle Street has not changed basically except for decor such as iron railings on the left in front of Castle House, and the Carriage house, and a wrought iron balcony above the Craft Shop.

We now take the left turn up to the motte and bailey mound situated on the right, opposite the Mount. This climb uphill was originally the narrow, steep road behind the railings on Castle Hill, beside the last house on the left. In the days of early freight vehicles they ground up the hill in bottom gear, while descending when loaded was equally hazardous, shuddering as the driver braked. This route was used by lorries carrying stone from local quarries during the construction of Clatworthy and Wimbleball dams. The new and present road towards Morebath and Watchet was cut through not so long ago. It is thought that this project filled in a secret passage between Castle House and the Motte. That is possible, but not confirmed.

Top: *The stables in Fore Street, c.1890 and,* above, *the same premises in 1910, then in use as a cycle store. The building is now Serenger's.* RK

Left: *Another view of Brook Street, this showing Queen Victoria's Jubilee celebrations in 1887.*

Below left and right: *Two photographs, taken by Gerald Burnett, showing the demolition of Staddon's on the east end corner of Serenger's shop, to widen the road. Tommy Hancock is standing nearest the camera* Photo from Kathleen Burnett

Left: *Staddon's corner, with two houses on the right being demolished to widen the road junction.* RK

Morebath Road continues with dwellings either side until a left turn takes you down Frog Lane and back into the town. Turn right at the bottom and you see Back Street, the scene of that captivating picture of Ann Challice and her donkey cart collecting 'any old iron'.

Back street was very narrow and Tommy Hancock is seen playing marbles with his friends. Rex Serenger told me that his mother, Pat Butler, is one of the girls watching Tommy. Either side of

the street is an Inn. The Angel, where Bampton Pharmacy is now, and The Lion, stood opposite.

The closure of the railway station made widening and straightening the top of Luke Street easy. Once the railway was filled in the sharp 'S' bend from South Molton road disappeared and the old bridge became one-way from High Street.

An old aerial view shows the original and present layout. West Street and Market Close were fields, with only a handful of cottages at the

Left: *Back Street, around 1890. The woman with the cart is Ann Challice. Tommy Hancock is the boy sitting in the road, facing the camera, and one of the two girls in white aprons is Pat Serenger (née Butler), who was to become Rex Butler's mother. Note the Red Lion Inn, first right, and the Angel Inn on the left.* RK

Below: *Widening the road in Back Street, 1975.* RK

Below: *A view up Fore Street c.1900, into Newton Square, where we see Gare's, chemist and druggist. The Angel Inn stands on the right. On the church is the single-faced clock.* RK

Above: *Bampton railway bridge looking down Luke Street, c.1900. The sign above the bridge reads 'Ride with caution'.* RK

beginning of West Street, and there were almost no houses up High Street, and no Barnhay or Industrial Estate, either.

The roads were rough, without tarmac. Many of the pictures show clearly the lines of the cart wheels pulled by horses. Scotts 'made' the roads in 1926, putting down a tarred surface. The first efforts were not so good as the tar and chippings stuck to the horses feet, and everything else!

Once a new machine arrived at Scotts, they were responsble for surfacing roads both locally and far and wide. Inevitably transport progressed from horse and cart to motor car, vans and traction-engine lorries. Motor lorries came on the scene and their size grew. The once narrow cart tracks could not cope, so widening at the expense of some properties, notably at Frog, Back, Castle and Fore Streets junction, began.

Top left: *Luke Street c.1910, looking down into Newton Square.* RK

Top right: *Neighbours in Frog Street, l-r: Bob Alderman; Alice Collard; Mrs Gillard, c.1940.* photo Eileen Shere

Above: *New Buildings c.1930.* RK

Above right: *Council houses in West Street, c.1960.* WI/Crutwell

Right: *A view taken from the church tower showing the new road layout at the junction.* BS

Looking down at St Michael and All Angels church from a garden in High Street. BS

Chapter 2 - The Church

From any hilltop, look down into Bampton and the square bell tower of the Parish church, St Michael and All Angels, will capture your attention. Unlike the single clock face of earlier times, two friendly clock faces, one on the east, one on the west wall, tell you the time. The new clock was installed in 1921, made by Smith's of Derby, with pleasant Westminster or Cambridge chimes accepted happily in everyday life by the locals, and sorely missed when silenced.

Mr Webber, whose grandaughter, Gladys, lives in Bampton now, was lowered down the front of the church tower in a cradle to fix the new clock. Mr Webber worked for William Nott & Son, the local builders. The previous clock had been there for almost two hundred years, made by Lewis Pridham of Sandford in 1728.

It is a church whose history goes way back to an earlier wooden building founded in the seventh or eighth century. The pre-Conquest church was linked with the monks at Glastonbury Abbey,

indeed one of their abbots, Bernwald, was buried underneath the high altar in Bampton. At the Conquest, William gave Bampton church to Walter of Douai, one of his knights. He in turn handed the church on to Bath Abbey. In the fifteenth century the church changed hands again, this time coming under the hand of Buckland Abbey, near Tavistock, in South Devon. A document dated 1444 states the abbey is to provide a Vicar and a house. The house was on the site of the old vicarage, seen today on the south side of the church. It is possible that an earlier rectory stood on the north side of the Church where a house has a doorway opening into the churchyard.

One of the early Lords of the Manor was a William Bourchier, whose family was to make a great impact on the town during the growth of the wool and cloth trade in the fifteenth century. The little pamphlet in the church gives an interesting picture of how an early settlement, long

Perhaps the oldest surviving photo of Bampton Church, dating from 1880. RK

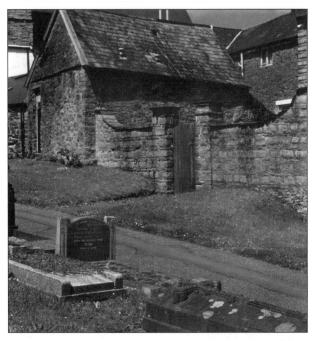

The door from a possible earlier vicarage, opening on to the churchyard from the back of Reg Kingdon's house. BS

before the Saxons arrived, was situated where Briton Street lies. This street lies between Batherm Bridge and the Seahorse Inn at the three-way road junction.

Two ancient trading routes crossed the river Batherm, and looking up Briton Street on your left, immediately as you leave the bridge, beneath you is part of the remaining cobbled road. Today Bampton is still on a crossroads, between Taunton to the east and Barnstaple in the west, while the Exeter-to-Minehead route runs north to south.

A new 'tun' or 'town' was built about AD 712, at Newton Square, along with a church. Many early churches were dedicated to St Michael, the Archangel, who threw down Satan. Such churches often stood on previous pagan sites and the oval enclosure, suggesting a pagan origin, can be traced around the present church, and both the old and the new vicarages.

It is thought that the first stone-built church appeared in the twelfth century, and traces of a window about that date remain high in the south wall, just east of the doorway. The tower and chancel followed in the thirteenth century.

As Bampton flourished in the fifteenth century the north aisle was built and the church was enlarged. At this time pillars and arches were built in stone brought to Bampton at considerable cost from the famous quarries at Beer, some 40 miles away. Cast your eyes up to the arches in the nave and notice the carved capitals, some are simply foliage, some are of angels holding books.

Bampton church and churchyard, c.1900. RK

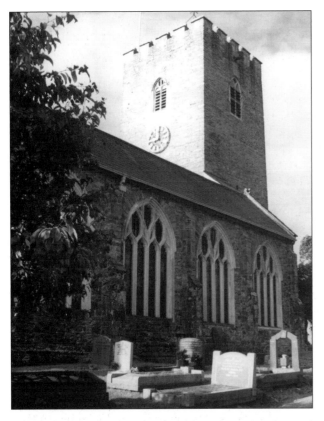

The church viewed from the north. Note the changed position of the clock face from earlier days. BS

while the one at the west end shows a fierce beast attacking four men, also holding books.

A typical Devon roof of oak, fashioned in the waggon-roof style, covered the whole church which is also well known for its beautiful oak rood screen separating the chancel and nave. Originally this screen would have been brightly painted with figures of saints in the panels, and in the rood-loft above the screen, there would have been carved figures of St John and Our Lady flanking the crucifix. The position of the screen has changed over the years, it being taken towards the altar where the screen was shortened to fit into the chancel arch in 1731. Later it was returned to the original position towards the end of the last century. The 'missing' ends were replaced much later, in 1938.

In 1872 the decision to save the decaying church was made. During the enormous task of thorough restoration the internal walls were stripped of plaster and white wash. The south wall was strengthened but still leans today. The restoration finished in 1898 with a celebratory public lunch and tea.

St Michael and All Angels always has a welcoming feeling and sunlight streaming through the windows enhances that feeling. Even on the saddest occasions and the coldest day there is a comforting feeling.

Looking east from behind the school - the newer houses with the church prominent. CS

Above: *Thought to be the oldest view of the interior of the church, c.1880. Note the position of the screen which was placed much further back than it is today.* RK

Left: *The interior of the church showing the magnificent waggon roof.* RK

Above: *The Flower Festival has always attracted great interest and support. Shown here, in 1972, l-r are: Geoff Chamberlain, Mrs Connell, Brian Chamberlain, Revd R.K.R. Coath, and James Connell.* RK

Top right: *Detail of the font which was brought from St Lukes Chapel in High Street. The font cover was carved by Eleanor Bennett.* BS

Right: *'Jack-in-the-Green' carved on the pulpit.* BS

Flower Festivals draw many visitors and the stone walls make a perfect backdrop for the wide variety of magnificent floral displays, painstakingly arranged by local volunteers.

Eleanor Bennett, who died in 1987 aged 104, carved the cover on the fifteenth century font, seen as you enter through the fourteenth century porch and latched double door.

Other notable features include the Jacobean oak pulpit, installed in the seventeenth century. Among its carvings there is a Jack-In-The-Green, an ancient fertility symbol, of which this is an unusually late example. In 1731 a gallery was built across the west end of the nave, and box pews were installed when the rood screen was moved into the chancel arch.

During restoration work some one-and-a-half centuries later, the nave roof was found to have pushed the south wall outwards, this had to be rebuilt and tied in. Out went the box pews and in came the benches we use today. Down came the gallery, and back to its original place came the screen. At this time the oak choir stalls were placed in the chancel.

Near the screen is the door giving access to the rood loft, and here also is a small piscina (washing vessel) where the Communion vessels would have been washed, indicating the presence of a small side altar here. There is another piscina on the south side of the sanctuary.

The window east of the door dates from about 1495. This window, complete with family arms in the bottom left-hand corner, was given by Lady Elizabeth Fitzwarren (whose maiden name was Dinham), and her second husband, Sir John Shapcote of Knowstone, a village a few miles to the west of Bampton.

The glass in this window was originally in the window behind the organ, near to where the Bourchier Family were buried. It was moved to serve as a memorial to the Bampton men who lost their lives in the First World War. Although the pieces were jumbled it is possible to see: 1. the Angel Gabriel telling Mary that she is to become

The lectern. BS

the mother of Christ. 2. Jesus ascending into heaven with his disciples watching. 3. St George slaying the dragon, and three figures representing the Trinity. The wonderful stained glass windows and the green-coloured glass replaced the plain glass windows in the eighteenth century.

There are two parish chests, both very old. The larger one is dated 1684, and bears the name of the churchwarden, John Bryant. The other is mediaeval. Church chests usually had three locks, one for the vicar, and with churchwardens holding the other two.

It was during the time of the first known vicar, Osmund, in 1258, that Bampton Fair was confirmed in a charter by Henry III, being held at St Luke's-tide, although now the Fair is always held on the last Thursday in October. A list of the vicars of Bampton Church, going back to Osmund, can be seen in the Chancel.

William Bourchier was influential in the cloth industry and was much involved with the church.

One of the many beautifully decorated kneelers made by Anne Bennett. Her designs incorporate symbols associated with the parish.

When he died he was buried elswhere but his family are buried inside the church. Two big altar-tombs, made of Cornish stone for Bourchier Family members, were demolished in 1770. The stone fragments were scattered but some were later put together on the wall beyond the Communion rail on the left side. A carved letter 'T', for Thomasine Bourchier, and the two Bourchier family badges, one of a reef knot and the other of a pair of 'water bougets', can still be seen.

As you climb up the steep stairs through the tower, it is the huge bells, six in all that take your attention. They have a wonderful tone in full peal, and an abiding memory for many locals is the sound of these bells, drifting over the village, welcoming in a New Year.

Thomas Bilbie of Cullompton recast the bells in 1800. In 1960 the tenor bell fell during a bell-ringing practice and all six bells were sent off by train from Bampton Station to Loughborough for retuning. They were returned to be rehung in May 1962 on a metal bell-frame, replacing the huge, weakening oak frame.

The bells are incredibly heavy, the lightest being the treble, which leads a peal, and is inscribed 'When I call follow me all'. The tenor weighs 15cwt, being the heaviest, more solemnly inscribed 'I to the church the living call, and to the grave do summon all'.

Parishioners love to hear the wonderful sound of Bampton's six bells in full peal. Visiting ringers from all over the surrounding area frequently come to our church and ring the bells, while their families walk around and look at the flowers in summer.

As you catch your breath from the exertion of your climb, and look out from the tower over Bampton, do not forget to note the weather vane which was given in 1808.

The fine organ we see today was installed early this century, having been planned-for during the restoration. A small band played for services prior to the organ installation.

Two very important ladies are remembered in our Church: Suzannah Webber and her sister Elizabeth Penton. Elizabeth started a school for fifty poor children in 1821, in what later became the National School in Brook Street. Suzannah started the Webber Charity for poor widows. A memorial to their parents is in the Church on the south wall near the lectern. A smaller plaque remembering the two sisters is on the north wall near the Organ.

The east end of the church is filled by a classical style altar piece, installed in 1816 to house a painting of Christ carrying a cross. This was given to the church and signed by local artist Richard Cosway who was born at Oakford, a village three miles from Bampton. Cosway was famed as a miniaturist during the eighteenth century.

Another painting given to the Church is by the Venetian painter Guiseppe Ghezzi. It shows the Holy Family about to cross a river on a ferryboat and is called 'The Flight into Egypt'

The carved roof bosses in the church take on many fantastic shapes, and one in the chancel roof shows the face of a man with his tongue hanging out.

The church was lit inside with oil lamps until 1926 when the Exe Valley Electric Company established themselves in Bampton, and twenty lights, costing £64.2s.0d, were fitted.

Step outside the lovely church and pause to look at the ancient yew trees. These have taken some buffeting from storms but have largely survived. Cattle grazed in the churchyard until the end of the nineteenth century and the stone jackets around the trees protected the trunk and prevented the animals nibbling at the very poisonous foliage.

Compare the exterior of today with the earliest photograph of about 1880 when the walls were plastered, giving a bleak aspect.

In the south wall, on a little stair turret, is a small sundial dated 1586. This is the earliest dated sundial in England.

Beside the Tower once stood some very old stocks. It is said that the people of Bampton were delighted to see the last-known person use them for being drunk. He was a William Copp, in 1862. Around the corner on the west wall of the tower is a memorial reading:

Bless my iiiiii's,
Here he lies,
In a sad pickle,
Killed by an icicle!

It is for a clerk's son who was killed by an icicle falling from the tower, in 1775.

The late Fred Webber, a keen gardener from Frog Street in the 1970s, donated 12 rose bushes for the main path in the churchyard. Maureen, his daughter, donated a further 24 bushes to help the churchyard to look good in the national final of the Britain in Bloom competition, 1998. Bampton has freqently qualified for the final and

Above: *An un-usual epitaph.* BS

Left: *The church and its ancient yew tree, c.1940s. In 1979 the tree was a victim of a storm; half of it was blown down and the remainder removed for safety reasons.* RK

has won the national title for Best Large Floral Village on four occasions since 1970.

It is all very well writing and producing pictures of our lovely old church of St Michael and All Angels, but to give real colour to the history of our church, you need people! Who better to start with than the Vicar.

Today Bampton Church is without a Vicar and it may be some time before a new one is appointed. The Revd Paul Ockford left us in the summer of 1998 to return to Yorkshire, but we are fortunate to once again have the support of a former vicar, of neighbouring Morebath Parish, the Reverend Tony Grosse. When the Revd Frayling died, Tony looked after our parish very capably and some parishioners hoped he might stay. However this was not to be and Tony moved to Hemyock until he retired to Bampton, living in a cottage with his wife, Eve, and their greyhound.

Three other vicars who should be mentioned from the long list in the chancel: the first is Osmund, the first known vicar of Bampton; the second is Bartholomew Davey, an extremely long-serving-vicar whose incumbency lasted from 1785 to 1841. It appears that an expanse of 56 years was a little too long for some folk for a story is told that one day the following note appeared nailed to the church door:

The passun is a wored out,
The Clerk is most ado,
The Sexton's gude for nort:
'Tis time to have all new!

Paul Ockford was only too pleased to see the story of our third Vicar, the Reverend Howard Frayling used in this book. Revd Frayling was a bachelor but he got deeply involved in the life of his parishioners, with sport as his chief interest. As long as you went to church you were able to play sport of great variety, simply because Howard organised a lot of it!

He was an active Scoutmaster and a photograph (below) from a Scout camp shows a young Ern Serenger (Rex's Father) boxing with Bill 'Cocky' Collard at Marsh Bridge.

Revd Frayling kept a donkey and when the first one died he bought a second one from Bickleigh. Bernard Kingdon, (Reg's brother) went by train to Bickleigh to collect the donkey which then had to be walked home, over ten miles.

A cry of help from Bernard at Tiverton told how the donkey refused to move another inch. Revd Frayling got in his little car and arrived in Tiverton to find the donkey with Bernard among a crowd of curious people. Howard went quietly up to the donkey, put his hand in his pocket and

Three views of the Revd Frayling. Above left: *a portrait photograph.* Photo courtesy Alan Collard. Left: *One of Julie Watson's 'Comic Cuts'.* Centre: *Riding one of his famous donkeys at the Vicarage in 1950.* Above: *Ern Serenger and Bill 'Cocky' Collard boxing at Scout camp at Marsh Bridge c. 1950.*

Above: *The vicarage seen across the lawns and tennis court, around 1940.* RK

Right: *Miss Frost, the Revd Frayling's housekeeper. c.1940.* RK

offered chocolate to the animal. A quick hee-haw and Bernard was off, heading towards home!

Revd Frayling usually had a good attendance at Matins as he cut the hour-long service to a crisp forty minutes, including a sermon. This meant that ladies could get home to cook the Sunday lunch.

A new organ was bought in 1913 for St Michaels and the parish has been fortunate to have two organists, whose combined service has lasted for 87 years: Miss Gertrude Vicary, 50 years, and Michael Rendell, who retired in 1995, after 37 years. Miss Vicary taught Michael to play the organ, and Michael played at Cove Church for eleven years before taking over at Bampton. It is a big commitment to be sole organist but both Gertrude and Michael managed cheerfully as it was 'part of the job'. Michael's job went further than organist as he became choirmaster too. He got on well with everyone as his quiet manner and expertise made choristers listen.

Some choristers Michael recalls from earlier years, in the 1940s are basses, Frank Smolden, Arthur Gibbings, Walter Cottrell, Geoffrey Brice, all basses; tenors Victor Burrows, Bob Smolden, Wilf Jefferies, Ern Serenger; and, mostly sopranos, Annie Cottrell, Peggy Langdon, Mrs D.M. Haste, and Margaret Hancock.

Choirboys included, Robin Blamey, Ern Kerslake, Bernard Kingdon, Dilwyn Cottrell and many others, although boy trebles were constantly changing as their voices broke. During the Second World War some of these choir members could only sing at Bampton when War duties allowed, many of them being in the Home Guard, Air Training Corps or Rifle Club, if not in one of the Armed Forces. All young men and women of the parish who were in the forces were entered on a list on the altar and remembered in prayers of the parish at each Service.

Bampton has been lucky to have a good choir at St Michael and All Angels. Today the numbers are low but, as the photographs show, many young people swelled the numbers in years past and may well in the future.

I can remember Wilf Jefferies as a sort of gentle giant as he appeared in his cassock and spotless white surplice, He was a man of many parts in the course of church work: chorister, bellringer, verger and server, to mention a few. But Wilf also worked on the railway at Bampton and took great pride in keeping it clean and tidy, with the garden his special interest.

Wilf Jefferies - a 'Comic Cut' by Julie Watson.

Bampton Parish Church Choir at a Rothwell wedding at Morebath c.1934. Back row l-r: Len Bowden; Vic Burrows; Ern Serenger; Wilf Jefferies; Charlie Broomfield; Frank Staddon; Frank Smolden. Boys l-r: Reg Kingdon; unknown; Ken Burnett; Ken Goodland; Alan Collard; Ern Gould; Derek Hagley; Hubert Taverner; Dilwyn Cottrell; Ern Kerslake; Dennis Oxenham. RK

Bampton Parish Church Choir, July 1965. Back row l-r: Reg Edwards (Choir Master); Michael Rendell (Organist); Stephen Edwards; Patrick Rendell; Geoff Chamberlain. Middle row: Denise Kingdon; Tony Gratton; Des Marley; Robin Woodman; David Tindall; Peter Bellamy; Brian Dunn; John Bellamy; Robin Davey; Jim Rycroft, Jean Davey; Helen Rycroft. Front row: Rosalind Nott; Vernon Kingdon; Stuart Coles; Tony Woodman; Phillip Venn; Paul Edworthy; Neil Strong; Yvonne Collard; Pauline Chamberlain. Reg Edwards and Michael Rendell worked together with the choir and organ until Reg's death when Michael took on both jobs. RK

Bampton Church bellringers at practice, c.1974. Clockwise from front: Yvonne Collard; Pauline Chamberlain; Margaret Gold (captain); Patrick Rendell; Reg Kingdon; Christopher Woodman; Barry Attwater. John Waite was Captain of the Tower before Margaret Gold took over.

ꞷ Other Places of Worship ꞷ

Other places of worship in the parish included, St Lukes Chapel, 200 yards from the church up at the top of the narrow High Street, where Grey Gables stands today. This was one of several small chapels (a few were private chapels), gone long ago. There was also a Baptist Church, built in Luke Street around 1690. It fell into decay but was rebuilt in 1860, later to become two dwellings, with the cemetery contained in the rear gardens. Arnold Seward remembered a Mrs Venner being the last person to be buried there.

The Methodist Church in Mary Lane celebrated its centenary in March 1962, having been built by the Bible Christians, and is very much alive today. One wedding of note from early this century was on New Year's Day 1909 when Jessie and Harry Sampson were married there. They shared their special day with the proclamation of the intro-duction of State pensions, and as the newly weds approached their waiting horse and carriage at the end of Mary Lane, opposite the Post Office, the

Bampton Methodist Chapel. Mary Lane, taken at the centenary in 1962. RK

Luke Street c.1900, with the Baptist Chapel on the left. RK

proclamation was being made by the Town Crier, Robert Webber. He walked across Brook Street to wish the couple a long and happy life and the hope of collecting their pensions in time to come.

Out of the town there were, and still are, several other places of worship. Some neighbouring churches have shared the vicar of Bampton, and this may change again when a new vicar is appointed. As long ago as 1107, people worshipped in St Petrocs chapel at Petton, four miles east of Bampton. This chapel was rebuilt about 1848 by the Troyte Family and is still used regularly.

St Katherines, up above Dipford farm, was reached by a narrow farm track at Shillingford, two miles east of Bampton. During the 1800s this little chapel fell into disuse but Dorothy Webber (later Seward) remembers, while living with her parents Fred and May Webber at Dipford Farm this century, how a service was held in the old chapel after she and her sister Kathy cleaned it out. By then the chapel was no more than a barn. Sally Luxton of Parsonage Farm, Petton, found the following in her scrapbook relating to St Katherines:

Davidson wrote in 1849, 'Service not performed for 14 years. Now a ruin. Last repaired in 1813, after which the east wall fell down. The piscina and bell were removed by the chapel warden. The bell lay in a barn for some years. It was bought at a sale at the farm [presumably Dipford] for one shilling and was placed in Morebath School oppo-

site the Church where it was used until the school closed in 1949, when it was taken to the new County Secondary School at Bampton, where it stands in the quadrangle.'

A further note believed to be written in 1916:

Still in use when John Staddon was a boy. John Staddon died in July 1937, aged 104 years. Parson Walker, curate of Bampton, was the last to perform duties there. Last funeral was that of a girl aged 12, whose mother lived at Ford in a cottage occupied by Stevens in 1916. Probably lack of funds brought it into disuse. It was then used as a barn. When later a move was made to have another place of worship on the same spot, Mr Rowcliffe, the owner of Dipford Farm on which the site was, opposed it and threatened to fight it if the case was brought.

All people who died at Ford were buried in the three-cornered burial yard at Shillingford. Once a month Parson Davey rode to Petton. That Sunday was known as 'Little Sunday' owing to there being no afternoon service. When he got to the top of Castle Street, the Clerk jumped up behind and 'Parson and Clerk' rode (on horseback) one behind the other to the Chapel).

A funeral at Petton Church which drew many mourners from across the parish, in 1976, was that of former Shillingford Headmaster Mr Herbert Ellis, who died in his early sixties.

The tiny Methodist Chapel near the bridge in Shillingford held regular services until much later.

Members of the Bampton Methodist Church leaving the railway bridge on their outing to Minehead, 1910. RK

Right: *Town Crier, Robert Webber proclaiming the start of the old age pension outside the Post Office on 1 January 1909. This coincided with the wedding of Jessie and Harry Sampson (Joy Coles' parents) at Bampton Methodist Church.* Photo Joy Coles.

Kathy and Ern Luxton's wedding at Bampton Methodist Church. Photo Sally Luxton

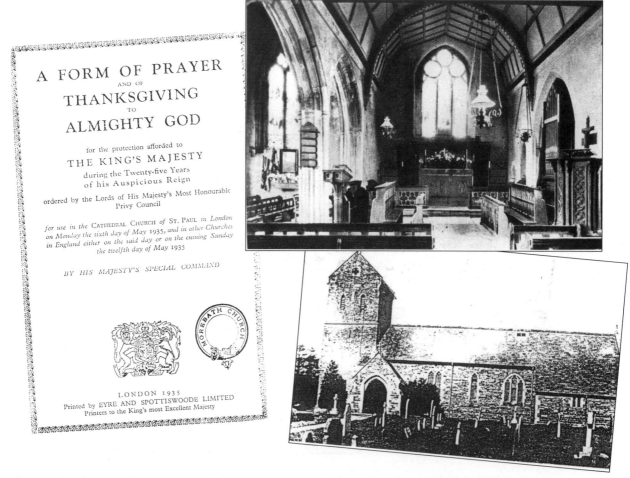

Above left: *Order of Service to celebrate the jubilee of King George VI at Morebath, May 1935.* Top right: *Interior of Morebath Church 1900.* Above right: *Morebath Church from an early photograph.* RK

Here Kathy Luxton (née Webber) and her mother, May Webber, both played the organ. Ken Vincent and his wife looked after the chapel until it closed.

Two other chapels were at Denscombe and Zeal. These last two had no dedications and disappear from the records by the 1400s.

For the fit and adventurous members of the Parish, there is an annual Four Churches Walk. Beginning at Bampton Church, the route takes in the parishes of Morebath, Clayhanger and Petton, who all share the *Signpost* parish magazine each month. The Vicar of Bampton is also shared by these parishes. A few years ago Huntsham came under the care of the Bampton vicar, too, while Morebath Parish was in the Exe Valley Group of Churches.

The Four Churches walk winds pleasantly along tracks, lanes and pastures to Morebath, to St George's church. Next comes a longer stretch heading east to St Petrock's, at Petton, with the final leg finishing at St Peter's in Clayhanger.

St. George's at Morebath has a keen team of bell ringers with Jim Vellacott as tower captain. The four bells, thought to have been in the Tower since 1553, were recast into five in 1742 and an extra bell was added in 1883. Like Bampton the bells have delightful inscriptions, including 'Prosperity to our Benefactors', and 'Peace and Good Neighbourhood'.

Vicar Christopher Trickey was a bit like the Vicar of Bray, as he used all ways to hold on to his job for fifty years during the Reformation. He kept the Church accounts and day-to day-running records in so meticulous an order that they have become famous books. Many clergy lost their-posts during this period so it was quite out of the ordinary that the Revd Trickey stayed so long. His name lives on in the village in Higher Trickeys, cottages.

At Christmas time Bampton church does not now hold a Midnight Mass, but Morebath does, so many people make the short journey to St George's. Its unusual saddle-back tower is

Far left: *Petton chapel, a drawing from the book* Chapels of the Tiverton Methodist Circuit, 1989.

Left: *Clayhanger Church.*

Below: *Sally Luxton's Bible Christian certificate of baptism.*

BIBLE CHRISTIAN CONNEXION.—BAPTISMAL CERTIFICATE.

No.	Child's Christian Name.	Parents'		Father's Rank or Profession.	Date and Place of Baptism.	By whom Baptized.
		Full Names.	Residence.			
79	Elizabeth Mary	Thomas & Martha Ann Mantle	Great Pill Bampton Devon	Farmer	May 14th 1882 Bampton Chapel Devon	Edmund T Turner

I certify that the above is a true copy of an entry in the Baptismal Register Book, No. *1* for the *Tiverton* Circuit.

Witness my hand this *14th* day of *May* 18*82*

Edmund Turner

thought to have been built about 1875, but Morebath people have been worshipping there for 900 years. The mixture of ages and styles throughout the structure make the Church special, but the oldest parts in evidence today are the tower and the base of the font.

Farming is essential to the way of life in this area and so harvest thanksgiving retains its genuine depth of feeling, and the words of the hymn 'All is safely gathered in, Ere the winter storms begin', has a special meaning.

The following stories of Petton and Clayhanger chapels and St Peter's Church, Clayhanger, were kindly written for me by Nicky Hayes of Clayhanger:

Petton Methodist Chapel sits beside the old A361 today but the first services were conducted in a cottage, then in a converted railway carriage. When this became too small it was decided to build a Methodist Church, in 1901. The land was given by H. Acland Troyte JP, and the stone was given by E. H. Denning JP. The total cost was estimated at about £250. Since then a new school room and kitchen, also a car park have been

added. Services are still held regularly on Sunday mornings.

Clayhanger Methodist Church was built in 1892 on a site which was formerly a shop and meeting house for Bible Christians, later destroyed by fire.

Services and Sunday School were held each week. Sunday School anniversaries were celebrated with games played in Nutcombe field. The Chapel closed in 1972 and converted into a dwelling.

From miles away you can see the fourteenth century tower of the ancient Church of St Peter in Clayhanger. Together with the sixteenth century manor house of Nutcombe they sit in a beautiful secluded valley some 800 feet above sea level. Inside the church some of the most striking features are the sixteenth century carved pew-ends. They include a man with a trident and a harpy, (a mythical monster with woman's head and body and bird's wings and claws.).

Behind the altar is part of the old rood screen and there is also an old oak alms box. The Norman font is built of Ham stone while the church itself is built from hard grey limestone.

Bampton National School, Brook Street, 1901. RK

Chapter 3 - School Days

Rural community life frequently revolves around the local school. Sometimes the village or hamlet is too small to support their own school and, sadly, this is presently the case with Shillingford. The school thrived for many years and local residents remember the happy days they spent there, until education budgets came under scrutiny and in the name of economics and progress, the axe fell on the school in 1992.

Bampton school was the alternative choice for primary education so the country children now duly arrived by school bus, making a long day for the five year olds.

In the past a child could receive all their education in Bampton. Most attended Bampton Primary School, the 'little school' and moved on to the Bampton Secondary School, the 'big school' at the age of 11 until the age of 16. Some, at the age of 11, went to the Tiverton Grammar School, until they reached 18 years of age.

Considering life in Bampton and the Parish

began somewhere about 2000 years ago our imaginations have to work hard until the late 1800s when photographs can back up our story of how things were. In this book we rely heavily on the photographs and records collected by Reg Kingdon. Some of his early photographs include several schools, some privately owned and others State run.

Today Bampton only has one school, in a building opened in 1938 as the Bampton County Secondary School. It was one of the first built in a quadrangle style, with pleasant gardens in the central area. The school bell came from St Katherine's chapel, now derelict, up behind Dipford farm at Shillingford. The bell stands today in the quad.

School days began for many local children in the 'little school', as it is fondly remembered. Miss Judith Coney, who was the last head teacher there, has kindly given the list of head teachers of the 'little school' since it opened in 1938:

The girls of Bampton National School 1898. Alan Collard's mother, is in the back row, third from the left.
Photo Alan Collard

Miss Winifred Cliff, Jan 1938—Dec 1956
Mr Reginald Edwards, Jan 1957—1968
Mr Harrison (acting), Sept 1968—April 1969
Mr Tregilges, April 1969—April 1973
Miss Mary Burnell, April 1973—April 1976
Mrs Anne Preston-Littlewood, April 1976—
    July 1982
Mrs.Margaret Trueman (acting), Sept
    1982—Dec 1982
Miss Judith Coney, Jan 1983—July 1992

Miss Coney recalled:

One notable event in the history of the 'little school' was the Nativity Play which was on television. It was staged I believe during Mr Edward's time, within the church, and was very successful. A good number of the readers of this book will have been in it.

Several local people helped to make the costumes and these were used for many following nativity plays. Even costumes we used for angels were originally from the famous nativity play.

Now a little of the school back ground also by Miss Coney:

Bampton 'little school' evolved from the free

school set up by Elizabeth Penton in 1821. The two Penton sisters have a tablet in their memory inside Bampton parish church. The 'little school' was a church infants' school housed in Mr Serenger's building in Station Road.

When the two new schools were built in 1938 I understand this school-building was used as a sunday school – the church owned the building at that time. Mrs Vodden remembers going to Sunday school there.

In the 1870s the National School opened and all the children over six years, I think, went there - the 'infants' (presumably the four to fives) stayed in the church school.

In 1938 the new Modern Secondary' and the new Church Primary school opened (the Primary opened on Jan 11th - the Secondary seems to have opened in 1937, but not officially until 1938).

The C E Primary took children from 5 to 11 and the County Secondary School took them from 11 to 16 (probably to 15 when it first opened, 16 in latter years of course).

From 1976 to 1992 the 'little school' became Bampton C.E. Aided First School, with children from 5 to 9 years. The 'big school' became Bampton Middle School (Devon County) and took children from 10 to 13 years.

Both schools closed in July 1992 (together with

Early School Days

Bampton Infant School, Station Road, 1901. RK

Early School Days

Bampton National School, Form 1, 1901. RK

Bampton National School, Form 3, 1901. RK

Early School Days

Bampton National School, 21 February 1911. Top row right to left: *F. Townsend (Headmaster); J. Knight; C. Baker; W. Blamey; Purnell; Chandler; F. Wensley; A. Gillard; Beedle; Miss Webb.* Second row from back r-l: *Florence Tooze; F. Milton; L. Cottrell; M. Harper; M. Tooze; Lee; Lucy Ware; E. Thomas; H. James; F. Baker; E. Weston; G. Brock.* Third row from back r-l: *Fred Tooze; E. Nott; Gladys Wensley (Birchdown); Nell Hegley; F. Chandler; B. Nott; G. Harper; Lily Chandler; Daisy Cottrell; Gertie Wensley; Ada Brook.* Front row: *Lee, Jack Blamey; James.* RK

A school report from Church Terrace School, Bampton, for Kathleen Webber, age 7, dated 1920. 'A really nice girl but a bit too indifferent.' RK

Shillingford) and a new school opened in September 1992 - a Church Aided School known as Bampton Voluntary Aided School, catering for children from Bampton, Cove, Shillingford, Stoodleigh, Oakford, but no longer the Rackenford children who had previously come to the Bampton Middle School.

Two notable headteachers were Charles Hulland and Michael Trueman, both highly regarded in the community and very committed to Bampton children.

School can be traumatic at first, both for children leaving Mummy, to be with strangers doing new things, and for the mother who does not know whether to be pleased or sad at the temporary parting.

Bampton has always been a good first step, and the head teachers have involved parents in many ways. Perhaps the favourite presentation, put on by the little ones, is the Nativity play. In the photographs of the early percussion band, there are those aprons again!

Many local people hoped the recently closed school premises would become a much needed community centre as it even had a swimming pool but the site was sold for building land and seven houses were built under the name of Winifred Cliff Court.

Miss Winifred Cliff was one strict and widely respected Bampton head teacher who grandparents of today will remember. Canes commanded respect for many years in many schools, and the odd blackboard rubber has been known to fly across a classroom, too!

Before Bampton had its present school buildings, schools were in various parts of the town. Although I can find no record of it, even Seward's Bakery was possibly a school in the past.

The present School has Mr Robert Tunley as the head teacher, and in keeping with present day standards, the curriculum followed gives many

Early School Days

Bampton Infant School, Station Road, 1927. A photograph taken in 1927. Back row l-r: *Mrs Napper (teacher); Cyril Chidgey; Jack Oxenham; Alan Collard; Dennis Broom, Besley; Norton Davey; Derick Venn.* Middle row: *Gilbert Gratton; Jack Gillard; Percy Hutchings; Amy Broom; Florrie Maunder; unknown; Weston; Greta Heido; Lucy Dart; Cissy Wood; Cyril Taylor, Chamberlain.* Front row: *Derek Hagley; unknown; Doris Cottrell; Gratton; Freda Coles; Doris Sulley; Rosie Hall; Jack Gould.* RK

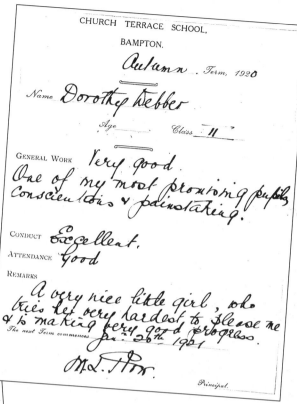

Left: Doris Staddon's report from 1919 from Bampton National School. Above: Dorothy Webber's report from Church Terrace School, 1920.

opportunities to primary age groups, both in and out of school time. All children who leave Bampton school can go to Tiverton High School where they have the opportunity to attend further education.

On 24 June 1976, Mrs E. Sampson officially opened a new classroom at the Primary School. The programme contained a lovely children's hymn. 'I love the sun, It shines on me, God made the sun and God made me.'

An interesting letter received by the author included memories of a former pupil at Bampton County Secondary School between 1952-57. It was written by Betty Berry of Rackenford, now Betty Morrish, who lives in Tiverton:

Bampton County Secondary School was known as one of the best schools in Devon. There was an interesting set of activities for each year. Year 1 We fed poultry and looked after the annual flower beds. Year 2 bi-annual flower beds. Year 3-4 options: rabbit and bee-keeping, flower arranging, and on Friday afternoons, picking anemones for selling at 1 shilling (5p). When the headmaster, Charles Hulland, sold off the rabbits, I bought a hutch for 2/6d (12p).

There were inter-school sports, visits to Rowe's farm, owned by a school governor, Mrs Olive Greenslade. Cheese and butter making classes were run by Miss Lloyd. We visited Taunton Museum, Foxes Factory at Wellington, Devon County Show and, if a film was worth seeing, we had a trip to Tiverton Cinema on the train.

We may not have had a piece of paper when we left Bampton School but we were young people who had good manners, common sense and a determination to do well in the world. Thanks to Mr Rundle, Mr Hulland, Mr 'Ticky' Lyons, Mr Clarke, Miss Wilson, Miss Armstrong and best of all Mr Bouquet! (who lived at Higher Lodfin, Bampton).

In 1956 because of lack of interest from local girls our headmaster asked for girls to enter the Carnival Queen Competition. The tickets were sold at 6d each and the ones for the under 11's were 3d each. We were given our dresses made by Mrs V. Parkhouse (Philip Venn's Grandmother), and Mrs Fowler, wife of Mr Albert Fowler who kept the fish and chip shop (the Fowlers were Dean Fowlers Grandparents). We also had a cash prize of £3. There was a Queen's Ball after the crowning ceremony and a few weeks later the Queen's

float headed the carnival procession which included Bampton Town Band. It was freezing cold and
I believe one of the band died at the end of the
parade, poor man. There were 10 floats and walking entries.

As usual the Rose Family took part, they came
from the Washfield-Stoodleigh area.
In the last Carnival Queen Competiton, run in
1957, Rosemary Bolt from Huntsham was the
Queen.

Building work underway on the new Secondary Modern School at Bampton, 1936-37. RK

Above: *The completion of both new schools in 1938.*

Right above: *One of the opening ceremonies for the
Secondary School, early in 1938. From left to right:
Alan Collard; the Secretary to the Governors; Revd
Frayling; County Council representative; Jago
Alderman.*

Right below: *The opening ceremony taking place in
the assembly hall, 1938.* all RK

School Days 1930s to 1950s

Bampton National School, Brook Street, 1931. Back row l-r: *Rosie Hall; Francis Rooke; Lucy Dart; Priscilla Ware; Olive Woodman.* Third row: *Mr Shenton (Headmaster); unknown; Madge Bowyer; Doris Sully; Christine Bowyer; Winifred Hancock; Eva Gregory; Rose Alderman; Doris Cottrell; Greta Heido, unknown.* Second row: *Jack Oxenham; Reg Yendell; Cyril Chidgey; Percy May; Ernest Gould.* Front row: *Derick Hagley; Dennis Broom; Allan Collard; Hubert Tavener; Gilbert Gratton. RK*

Bampton Infant School, Station Road, Percussion Band, 1934. Back row l-r: *Geoffrey Brice; Winnie Webber; Laura Yendell; Hazel Gould; Suzette Haste; Vera Kingdon; Vera Stoneman; Joyce Willis; Albert Cottrell; Sid Coles.* Front: *Gerald Vicary; Roberts; Clifford Lazarus; Joyce Taylor; Fred Hutchings; Lorna Broom; Thelma Lockyer; Arthur Pinn; Caroline Roberts; Joan Hutter; Evelyn Eames; Pearl Roberts; Ray Kingdon; Jean Blamey; Marion Todd; John Chamberlain; Ken May; Clifford Cottrell (Conductor). RK*

School Days 1930s to 1950s

Pupils at Bampton Secondary Modern School, 1948.

Bampton Primary School 1957-8, Senior Class. Back row: *Reg Edwards (Headmaster); Helen Collard; Carol Chivers; Linsey Hill; Sally Herbert; Maureen Webber; Jane Rendell.* Third row: *Angelina Coles; Petronella Bouget; Wendy Crooks; Marilyn Marley; Leslie Glass; Margaret Gold; Carol Pittey; Leslie Thomas; Margaret Gardner.* Second row: *Barry Denner; Keith Cleave; Pauline King; Maureen Hartshorne; Marion Penney; Elsie Groover; Alison Appleby; Graham Matthews; Ray Hutter.* Front: *Richard Hill; Richard Davey; Peter Holland; Dennis Hutter; Phillip Rycroft; Mervyn Hancock; Christopher Hawkins; David Pershouse.* Photo Alan Collard

School Days 1930s to 1950s

Bampton Primary School, Netball Team 1957-8. Back row l-r: Marilyn Marley; Carol Pittey; Linsey Hill; Helen Collard; Ruth Laramy (teacher); Leslie Thomas; Carol Chivers. Front row: Leslie Glass; Marion Penney; Wendy Crooks; Petronella Bouget; Maureen Hartshorne. Photo Alan Collard

School Days 1960s to 1970s

Bampton County Secondary School 1965. Among those in the picture are: M. Marley; R. Pincombe; L. Lyons; Derek Mounce; Andrew Seatherton; W. Cooke; Allan Manning; Peter Cole; Jane Hancock; Rosemary Carter; Ruth Isaac; Derek Carter; Colin Tidball; Michael Ayres; Gary Appleby; Mary Edge; Valerie Down; Margaret Fisher; Jean Dennis; Paula Kingdon; Lynn Crooks; A Shere; J. Cottrell; A. Cornish; Anne Kerslake; Miss Jordan; Colin Smith; Colin Gunny; S. Chamberlain; Patrick Rendell; Alan Biddlecombe; George Kingdom; John Cottrell; John Sahanik. RK

School Days 1960s to 1970s

Bampton CE Primary School Football Team, 1971. Back row l-r: Richard Turner; T.S. Coldridge (teacher); Brian Chamberlain; Jonathan Routley; Ernie Blake; Stephen Balmforth; Michael Kelland; Brian Vodden; Grahame Beer. Front row: Lance Gould; Brian Kelland; Christopher Woodman; Michael Cottrell; Jonathan Smith.

Bampton CE Primary School Netball Team, 1971. Back row l-r: Teresa Waite; Cherry Gale; Paula Rowlands; Della Tucker. Front row: Penny Attwater; Christine Vodden; Jacqueline Bolman; Debbie Blackwell; Linda Alexander.

School Days 1980s to 1990s

The retirement of Kath Woodman from Bampton 'Little School'. The children include: Mark Hill; Tom Raffield; Christopher Caunter; Robert Adams; Adam Cox; Anthony Chambers; Luke Pickard; Saffa Falsafi; Matthew Heywood; Emma Greenslade; Sophie Scott; Mark Weston; Jan Loades; Aaron Weiss; Jessica Record; Richard Chambers; Jennifer Brice; Stacey Bristow; James Powles; Joanne Kingdon; Kim Williams; David Cleverley; Ryan Cox; Stacey Robinson; Tracey Nevill, Rosie James; Paula Taylor; Jennifer Law; Gemma Bristow; Diana Beales; Daniel Law; Victoria Cockram; Mark Penfold; Ben Atkins; Deborah Penfold; Ian Martin; Lizzie Record; Kimberly Bolt; Rebecca May; Ryan Nevill; Christopher Hill; Emily Malpass; Laura James; Timmy Kenny. RK

Mrs Preston-Littlewood's retirement as Headteacher of Bampton First School, 1982. l-r: Margaret Christie; Olive Greenslade; Mr and Mrs P-L; Revd D. Claridge; A. Mowll; Hilary Moreton. RK

School Days 1980s to 1990s

Staff and pupils at the 'Little School', 1986. Staff l-r: Mrs Salter; Miss Coney; Mrs Cottrell; Mrs Vodden; Mrs Chamberlain; Mrs Woodman; Mrs Aldridge; Miss Tomlinson. Pupils include: Joanne Venn; Alsion Blackmore; Andrew Bartram; Lee Cottrell; Craig Pope; Steven Fisher; Ian Martin; James Cleverley; Anne Marie Southcott; Katie Saunders; Tanya Povey; Lizzie Record; Angela Medland; Shane Pook; Sonia Povey; Laura James; Amanda Pook; Ruth Powles; Sarah Glidden; Annabelle Davies; Tanya Dagge; Emma Southcott; Dean Marley; Edward Mock; Neil Weston; Julie Lee; Daniel Law; Rachel Hill; Robert Parkman; James Cox; Julie Leigh; Yvonne Jackson; Claire Martin; Kimberley Bolt; Shelley King; Tim Jackson; Lucy Kenny. Photo M. Aldridge

Left: Staff and friends attending a farewell dinner at the Courtyard to mark the closing of the Little School, 1992. Photo Miss Coney

Right: *The demolition of Bampton Primary School 1997, looking up towards the 'Big School'.* BS

The Bampton Water Committee, c.1875, taken at the back of the White Horse Bampton, Back row l-r: *William Williams; Fred Townsend; Fred Seward; John Penwarden; John Thomas; Wilf Kingdon; William Davey; John Charles Rockett.* Middle row: *Frank Staddon; William Escott; Robert Webber; William Nott; William Blamey; Samuel Hoare.* Front row: *Frank Gibbings; Ted Rowe; Samuel Gibbings; Charles Davey.*

Chapter 4 - Parish Amenities

The Wishing Well Cafe, now a private residence started breakfasts every saturday in the summer about 4am and coaches filled the large carpark to overflowing. The Wishing Well was built by Fred Napper as a bungalow after he built the Shillingford Road Garage and then the bungalow that now goes with the garage business.

Holiday traffic often queued to get through Bampton from the Wishing Well in the east and from Gumbland Farm in the west. The police frequently had extra staff to try and keep things moving, but to cross Newton Square one could either wait twenty minutes at a time or take your life in your hands, put up your hand, hope the cars would stop, and run across!

Of course Bampton had no big car park so the town did not gain from passing trade at weekends, and the holdups were due to the narrow roads and sheer volume of traffic.

The complication and cause of hold-ups was that Fore Street was a two-way system, and at the four-way junction, and in front of the chemist shop, wide caravans and lorries could not pass easily. Also Traffic wanting to turn right into Brook Street from Fore Street got perilously close to having their bonnets shaved by through-traffic.

The former police station was on the right as you look south over the river bridge, and there used to be a Youth Hostel adjoining the river bridge on the right hand side. When these both closed the buildings were sold and turned into private dwellings.

The lovely old Vicarage, scene of many fetes over the years, is now also a private house belonging to Dr Mew. The vicar has a new vicarage next door.

Devon has many remote areas where the delay in getting a road ambulance could be fatal. None is more remote than Exmoor, and for outlying farms the Devon Air Ambulance is often called. This year the service which relies on public donations has increased its availability to seven days a week. The familiar red helicopter recently visited Bampton Primary school and the children thoroughly enjoyed meeting some of the crew and peeping inside the aircraft.

Every community needs a Hall and Bampton has two. A third one, the Central, at one-time the Gospel Hall, in Back Street, is nowadays a private dwelling. The Drill Hall, so named because the Territorials used to train there, was later renamed the Public Hall. It sits beside the river Batherm and serves as the indoor rifle range, offering two rooms upstairs for meetings. St Michael's Community Hall, built in the 1920s, was the Church Institute for many years, and even longer ago it housed stray animals according to some accounts. It certainly was a stable with a loft. This hall has recently been modernised and will gain further improvement through a grant from a National Lottery.

Both halls share regular bookings for local clubs and organisations. Short-mat bowling and American line dancing are two new introductions to local life.

WATER SUPPLIES

Consider the panic that sets in each time there happens to be a hiccup in the services we all take for granted today. When the electricity supply blinks it's all moans and groans, usually because someone has to miss the latest soap opera episode of *Emmerdale* or *Coronation Street* on television! Fortunately the water and sewage systems fail least of all. One can only marvel at the patience and hard work each day must have brought to running the home before the advent of such amenities.

If there was a settlement here in the sixth century, what happened to all the sewage? Where did the water come from for everyday use? Certainly the river provided water and possibly took away the sewage in the earliest days. We know that the Shuttern Brook ran open through what is now Brook Street, meeting the Batherm at what was a ford on the old trading route, just as it does today. Wells would have come much later! Imagine hauling every drop by bucket, for indoor or outside use. It is said that women are the stronger sex - in those early days they had to be!

Until 1871 wells, natural springs (or the river), were the only source of water in Bampton. A spring beside South Molton Road was piped at the expense of Mr J.C. Phillips of Silver Street, down to Newton Square. Bampton residents paid for a

One of the oldest surviving water taps in Bampton stands in Newton Square, next to one of a pair of red phone boxes that have been retained. BS

tap to be sited there and other taps provided supplies outside The Swan, Manor Mill, and the Toll House.

An emergency tank built of bricks with a cement lining was situated on the Station Bank opposite the Swan Hotel, where the public conveniences stand today (decorated with hanging baskets during the summer).

This tank helped out in water shortages. Later the water was pumped to another storage tank at the top of High Street, where Grey Gables looks down on to the town. This was the reservoir, excavated by Scotts and it still feeds the Bampton supply today. The photograph on page 50 shows the Water Committee with the stop cock keys and other tools probably soon after the first water installations.

Until early in the twentieth century everyone managed with this communal system. After that time individual houses began to appreciate the luxury of indoor supplies. Take a good look at the clothes worn in all the older photographs in this book, and try to imagine the toil of collecting water for washing them. Added to that chore was to heat enough water for the job, too! Materials were thick and heavy, no poly-cottons or viscose, so drying was yet another major task.

Even during modern times it has not been unknown for a stream of brown water to flow through the system, causing all sorts of frustration when white washing was found to be anything but clean in automatic washing machines!

ELECTRICITY

Houses and businesses were lit with oil lamps for centuries. Note them in the photos of early street scenes, and in the church. Public electricity supplies came in during the early decades of the twentieth century, and power for the first street lights in Bampton was produced from a shed behind Sewards bakery in Newton Square. The shed contained an engine that charged 100 batteries, giving enough power to light the first few street lights in the town.

Domestic electricity supplies came in 1926, when the Exe Valley Electric Company established themselves in Bampton. Homes were able to link up for the huge sum of one shilling per week (5p). For this amount two lights could be powered, but if you tried to light a third one at the same time, all power was lost!

Television came much later, sadly at the expense of many family get-togethers when people talked and entertained one another, especially during long winter evenings. Arnold Seward recalls Mr Walford, who had a wooden leg, bringing silent films to the Drill Hall and Gospel Hall in the 1920s. A pianist accompanied the films.

A resident recalls how early television brought a crowd of youngsters into their house to watch Roy Rogers or Hopalong Cassidy serials. The first TV sets were available in Bampton for the coronation of Queen Elizabeth in 1953.

Bampton has never been linked up to main gas supplies although many people use bottled gas in their homes, delivered or collected from local suppliers. The gas travels many miles for this purpose from Bampton Gas in Newton Square, and from Kings and Serengers, while most local garages also sell bottled gas.

SEWAGE

Many houses had cess pits in their gardens and it is believed raw sewage did not run through the open Shuttern Brook in Brook Street, although no one can be sure. An extract from records headed, Bampton Local Board, April 6th 1886, notes:

Sanitary Requirements: arising out of the minutes remark was made on the sewer gratings of Castle Street, and on the motion of Mr Periam seconded by Mr Chard, the surveyor (Mr Searle) was directed to flush all the sewer traps in the district once a week and to provide two galvanised buckets for the purpose.

So where did it go? The present treatment site for Bampton sewage was built at West Street, and prior to that the sewage ran into a cement tank in the field next to the Drill Hall.

Odd odours were smelt when a westerly wind blew off the modern treatment plant in the early days, but thankfully that fault was sorted out.

DOCTORS

Arnold Seward recalled a Mr Attwater, living in Great Court, who, although not a qualified dentist, would pulled out an aching tooth for you! He was Alec Attwater's grandfather. Great Court was an L-shaped row of cottages where the Public Hall car park is today. (In the small garden beside The Great House Inn, where Mr L. White had his barber's shop, was a cottage that you entered by going down two steps. This cottage was flooded every year.).

Dr Bovey had a surgery in Castle Street early this century. Other, later, GPs included Dr E.D. Morgan whose surgery was up the slope at Winslade House in Briton Street. Prescriptions were made up there, too. An early photograph shows a row of thatched cottages where the present garden stands in front of Winslade house. Dr Morgan was a well-respected gentleman who frequently sported a bow tie. He later moved house to live at Fairby on the way to Tiverton. This move allowed his junior partner, Dr Anthony S. Baker (Tony to many), to come and live in Bampton with his wife, June, in 1957. Later on their children, William and Paula were born here.

Tony Baker became one of Bampton's most popular residents and he eventually took over the practice from Dr Morgan.

Home births were equal in number to hospital births during that time. An expectant mother had one-to-one treatment from the midwife who lived locally and who stayed with her patient during labour, only summoning the Doctor in time for the actual delivery.

Bampton Parish has always been lucky to have a medical practice where the doctor would do house calls day or night. During Dr Baker's term, antibiotics and preventative vaccines became routine for children whose parents wished to have them used. He hit the local headlines quite early in his job at Bampton, although he modestly played the event down when asked to talk about it. Tony recalled:

I was called out one dark, winter night to the big bend in the River Exe, below Exeter Inn. A courting couple had accidently let the handbreak off in

Retiring after 32 years as a GP in Bampton, Dr Tony Baker is presented with an inscribed salver by Reg Kingdon, while attended by the first and last people he delivered as babies: two-month old Ben Lewis (held by his mother Sarah) of Shillingford, and Brenda Hayes (second right) of Dulverton. Also in the picture are June Baker (third right); five year old Steven J. Kingdon (centre), and Lt-Col. Maurice Wood (far right).

their car as it was parked on the opposite side of the road in a quarry. Seconds later they were in the river calling for help. Emergency services arrived. There was nothing I could do but watch, with an intuition that all might not go to plan, as the fire engine and crew from Bampton attempted to put a ladder across the water to the car from the field of Holmingham Farm. I went downstream and watched.

Fireman Les Woodman volunteered to crawl across the extended ladder to the couple. The man came back with no problem but as Les helped the girl across the ladder the extension parted from the main ladder, throwing both people into the water. Les scrambled ashore and I just caught the girl as she was swept my way by the river. It was Les who was the hero, not me.

However both Dr Baker and Les were given the Royal Humane Society Award for Valour, for their involvement.

Dr Baker retired in 1989 from general practice, and it was fitting, as childbirth had been a large part of his work, to see the first and last baby Tony had brought into the world share a presentation for their doctor. Local historian Reg Kingdon made the presentation speech. Today Tony Baker is almost as busy, sitting on various medical boards throughout the region.

His junior partner, Dr Chris Mew took over the practice and since then Bampton has become fortunate to have its own Health Centre, built in Barnhay under Chris's guidance. Dr Mew has Dr Paul Backhouse as his junior partner and Bampton patients still can have a night visit if necessary.

These days maternity cases and many patients needing hospital treatment are referred to Tiverton Hospital where the atmosphere is friendly and relaxed. Otherwise patients travel to the newly built Royal Devon and Exeter Hospital at Wonford where beds are always at a premium due to the huge area they service. It is hoped that one day Tiverton will have a new hospital.

Bampton's GPs and their families continue, as Tony did before them, to be involved in the community. Dr Mew has served on the Town Council while Dr Backhouse, who enjoys sport, runs in the annual Bampton 10-kilometre road race.

VETERINARY SURGEONS

Bampton does not have a full time veterinary centre in the town but it does have a surgery each day from Monday to Friday. The Dulverton practice of Elliott and Fieldhouse visits each afternoon and do house calls any time of the day or night if an animal is in distress.

Mr Newton was the local vet in the 1930s and, as the practice was in Newton Square, and the vet did not own a car, Arnold Seward used to take him by car on house calls when he finished work.

Today the site is occupied by Stuart Bennett, trading as Caxtons, a printer, and the veterinary practice is halfway down Brook Street in a cottage on the right, next door to Well House. An old milestone from the packhorse route days stands near the door.

FIRE SERVICE

Several years ago, when some old buildings were being demolished behind where today Kings, the agricultural suppliers are in Back Street, local garage owner, John Record spotted something of local interest and value. The previous owners had filled two large wooden boxes with tools and nails to bursting point. It was the writing still clearly seen on the side of the boxes that caught John's eye. It read: 'Bampton Urban Council'- the owners of the first wooden fire engine. These boxes had been fixed to each side of the engine to hold the water hoses. This fire engine was hand-pumped by six men and pulled by two horses. Sadly the wooden engine was chopped up for firewood in the 1960s. One tale remembered of those days goes like this:

The horses were kept in Lords Meadow, a field some way below the Fire Station, at the entrance off West Street [Hookins Oils and Tim Coles, agricultural engineer, are presently sited at Lords Meadow]. *As soon as the fire alarm was raised by maroon, the two horse jumped out of the meadow and galloped up to the station, ready and waiting for the firemen.*

Arnold Seward remembers the first hand-pumped engine also being kept at the Tiverton Hotel under the care of a Mr Miles, presumably before it was moved to West Street.

Another interesting snippet of information is how between 1920-25, when the firemen were summoned by a maroon being fired, the person in charge was the Rural District Surveyor, a Mr Monson, who lived at Barnhay House. As there was no telephone connected to his house (the first one in Bampton came in 1922), news of a fire came by word of mouth, or by a person on a bicycle.

Bampton firemen 1947. Back row l-r: *Charlie Sowden; Harold Caunter; Don Tarr; Gilbert Hutter; Frank Parkman.* Front row: *Len Gratton; Jim Ware; Jack Herniman; Jim Yeo; Frank Tarr; Joe Chamberlain.* RK

Bampton firemen 1998. Basck row l-r: Robert Strong; Robert Waite; S. Hutter; Neil Hawkins. Front row: *K. Pope; Tim Jackson; Tamara Barker.* BS

Mr Monson was the grandfather (on the maternal side) of Captain Brian Labbett, Retd, who lives in Bampton, at Bourchier Close, today. Brian told me:

My grandfather was a chorister and bellringer as well, as being in charge of the maroon at Bampton during the five years he lived here, having come for his work as surveyor. He retired in 1925 and moved to Hove where he continued his church combination of chorister and bellringer.'

Here is another story dating from 9 March 1886:

On returning from a fire at the chemist, oil and colour merchants at Dulverton, the Bampton Fire Brigade had a mishap near Coombehead about a mile from Bampton. The horses, driven by Mr W. Yendell, were rounding the point at High Cross when the engine slipped on a sheet of ice and was thrown towards the hedge. Some of the occupants were jerked off and injured by the fall, a labourer named John Salisbury breaking one of his ribs. Mr Robert Trickey, landlord of the Swan Inn received a cut on the head and Mr E. Hobbs watchmaker, strained his back. The party walked to Bampton and there Salisbury was attended by Mr T.A. Guinness, surgeon.

No mention is made of the fate of the poor horses!

Over the years Bampton has produced first class teams of firemen who have rightly been proud of their fast turnout times. In bygone days the siren was enough warning to locals to stand clear as the engine roared through the town, bell ringing furiously. Next came the klaxon, but today firemen are 'bleeped' with electronic alarm calls and the fire engine sports a wailing siren similar to the ambulances, a little confusing for residents, especially children, who turned out to watch the engine roar past, blue light flashing on the roof. It wasn't that many years ago when one fireman

SCENES FROM SEWARD'S FIRE 1988

had to manually ring the bell, even more exciting for the youngsters to see.

During the War a Scott's 6-ton lorry towed the fire trailer with the six-man hand pump, and later a Chrysler car towed the trailer pump, both being painted wartime grey.

In 1947 Les Woodman joined the Bampton Fire Service. The Station Master was Jack Herniman, while other firemen were Jim Yeo, Frank Tarr, Jimmy Ware, Gilbert Hutter, Charlie Sowden and Joe Chamberlain. A maroon still summoned the crew and sparked the horses into action.

Les served in the Fire Service for 37 years, being the longest serving junior officer in the county. He served in three different brigades, at Bampton: The National Fire Service, which was taken over by Devon County Fire Brigade, and later to become Devon Fire Brigade.

From Newton Square, then at West Street (Lords Meadow), next to High Street, the Fire Station later moved to its present home, Barnhay.

Les and many of the other firemen have seen all kinds of service. He has been Commended for scaling Bye Lane Quarry face to rescue two lads out rook egg hunting. He and present Station Officer Tony Williams pulled a resident out of a house fire in Brook Street. The person had no pulse but Edward Tanner, using brand new resuscitation equipment, saved the resident's life.

Another major fire occurred in 1988 at the Bakery and Spar Stores in Newton Square. Maybe the fire station should have stayed in the Square, as this property has had its fair share of trauma this century. First it was damaged by arson which exploded a dynamite store in the then wheelright's business next door. Part of the roof blew off and extensive damage occurred. The winter of 1946-47 saw the bakery catch fire. This was during a severe winter when the two bakers travelled to Dulverton each day, with chains on their vehicle, to bake Bampton bread in a brand new bakery lent to Arnold Seward, by Mr Pike.

In 1988, had the worst fire not happened in the day time, the author's family and all their pets would probably not be alive today. Bampton Brigade arrived with two crew ready in breathing apparatus (a new regulation) to find the youngest son, Richard Seward had escaped by a mere twenty seconds, while two cats had died in the lounge. Four Fire Brigades, Bampton, Dulverton, Tiverton and Witheridge, fought to save the building, causing mayhem in Newton Square on a rain-soaked May Spring Bank Holiday weekend. But it was the prompt turnout of Bampton Brigade, under the leadership of Ray Marley, that

undoubtedly saved the day. Although the front of the premises escaped visual damage it took four months for the rest of the house to be rebuilt and made habitable.

When things cannot get much worse sometimes it is best to laugh, and a friend arrived at the height of the fire to spend the holiday with the author's family. The friend, Dave Greenhalgh threw open his arms to embrace his friends surrounded by yellow oilskinned firemen declaring, 'You always give me a warm welcome but don't you think you have gone a bit too far, this time?'

The Bampton Crew have attended most of the major fires in Tiverton and surrounding district.

POST OFFICE AND TELEPHONE

An important stride into modern times came to Bampton on 9 May 1922, with the introduction of the telephone. The first exchange was in the room at the back of the present Post Office. The Post Office archives show, in 1924, telephone number 1 at Bampton Call Office; number 2 was Geoffrey Aspinall of Cove House; number 3 W. Blamey, General Stores; number 4 T. Fisher Physician and Surgeon, Winslade; number 5 Capt. Kennard, Wonham; number 6 J.W. Scott and Sons; number 7 F T. Seward, Produce Merchant 33, Brook Street; number 8 W. Stone General Merchant Luke Street; number 9 H. Tate Druggist Arms; number 10, Escott & Co. Baker and Confect., 2 Brook Street.

The coming of the telephone was a great asset to modern life. The service first came to Bampton in 1922, at the present Post Office. The switchboard used to put callers through and employed many people for that purpose. A call could be quite a lengthy process. Lilian Edworthy, then Lilian Yeo, worked at the switchboard and recalled:

In 1945 I started work at the Bampton Post Office, and at that time the telephone exchange, sorting office and Post Office counter were all in one room, where the existing Post Office is today. The Postmistress was Mrs. Cissy Coles, sister of Gilbert Todd ('Toddy') the chemist.
The telephone exchange was manned from the time the early mail came in until 10pm. Then a switch transferred the call bell to ring in the Postmistress' bedroom, or anyone who was on duty sleeping on the premises. They had to get out of bed and answer the caller. We did not get many 999 calls in those days.
In 1947 the telephone exchange was moved to

one of the back rooms of the Post Office and was manned 24 hours a day. It remained there until the exchange went automatic.
On the night of Seward's fire the exchange could not be roused so someone fetched the Brigade on foot!

Lilian and her sister, Doris Perry, both live in Bampton. Lilian and her husband Fred, who worked on the railway, kept the fish and chip shop in Newton Square, where the library is today.

These days Bampton has one of the most up-to-date automated exchanges, situated in Frog Street. In the same amount of time as it takes to call somone next door, you can dial and be speaking to someone across the world, with no loss of clarity.

Bampton has been fortunate to keep two of the older style red telephone boxes, one in Newton Square and one in Briton Street.

While rural areas of great scenic beauty are trying to find a way to hide power and telephone lines underground, the introduction of the mobile phone has brought some councils under pressure to allow somewhat unsightly pylons to be erected on skylines to ensure better reception.

The present Bampton Postmaster is John Gullidge whose mother Madge and Aunt Christine came to Bampton with their father and mother, the Bowyers, in the 1920s. Mr Bowyer came to install machinery at Scotts and the family stayed in Bampton, where both girls got married. Chris married Michael Rendell who worked at Scotts and became organist and choirmaster at St Michael and All Angels. Madge married Bert Gullidge. Madge is seen as Postmistress in one of the photographs.

The Post Office used to be across the street where Haircare is now sited, and also where the fish and chip shop is, before settling in its present position. John and his wife Carol have two daughters, and John has been a regular player in the past for Bampton Football Club.

John used to be the main newsagent, getting up early to sort hundreds of daily papers, although he was used to this as sorting the mail was also done at Bampton. You could post a letter in the morning and get it delivered in the town in the afternoon, with the Bampton post-mark on it.

Apart from the main amenities in any village or rural area other functions are necessary, from local government to recreational facilities. Bampton has it's own Town Council, at the time of writing with a lady chairman, Mrs Anne Sanders. Anne was elected to replace another lady chairman, Mrs Pat Brown. These two ladies followed the footsteps of Doris Gould who was the first lady to hold this office.

Bampton Town Council, 1998. Back row l-r: *Lillian Edworthy; Rex Serenger; Brian Seward; Peter Bage; David Burgess.* Front row: *Pat Brown; Anne Sanders (Chairman); Geoff Symons (Clerk); Diana Thomas; Phyllis Marley.* BS

The Council meet once a month and Bampton has a representative through the Shuttern Ward elected to sit on the Mid Devon Council. At present Peter Burgess holds this post. (Peter keeps bees and was called in to deal with a swarm on a roof in Castle street).

One of the tasks of the Bampton Town Council is to share out the Bampton Fair Day toll money between local organisations who request financial support to improve their facilities.

POLICE

Unfortunately Bampton does not now have a resident policeman. The old police station used to have its own sergeant and a constable, plus one in Oakford and one in Shillingford.

PC Cornell once lived with his family in Shillingford and a recent letter from the Ven. Tony Tremlett, Archdeacon of Exeter, to Margaret Baker of the old police house in Shillingford, was most interesting:

A man of many parts. Peter Burgess is seen here removing a swarm of bees from a roof in Castle Street. Photo D. Burgess

Dear Mr and Mrs Baker,
It was kind of you to let me drop in unannounced the other evening and to see inside of my grandfather's former house. I promised to let you have copies of the photographs: one is of my mother, and the other of Mr and Mrs Tremlett and their daughter, Freda. Both taken in 1933.

PC Tremlett and his daughter (on motorcycle) outside the police house in Shillingford in 1933. Mrs Tremlett stands in the doorway. Photo Ven. T. Tremlett

Resident's tales suggest PC Tremlett was not a person to cross! Freda Tremlett, his wife, worked at Seward's.

With increasing traffic came the increased problems with parking. At this time Police Sergeant Vernon was appointed to Bampton and the effect was immediate! Park anywhere you should not and you would not do so again! However, as in all things, he was firm but fair to all transgressors.

Above: *Freda Tremlett, daughter of PC Tremlett, outside the police house in Shillingford. Note the 'Devon Constabulary' sign over the door.* Photo Ven. T. Tremlett

Above right: *The new police house (left) and fire station at Bampton, taken shortly after their opening.* WI

Right: *Photos of the Youth Hostel, adjacent to the old police station.* Photo Mrs Currie

Chapter 5 - Bampton in Business

Bampton has been described as a thriving and self-sufficient town since its earliest beginnings, and this story continues today. While many rural communities are losing their local facilities, Bampton still offers a wide range, and thankfully the residents continue to support them. Certainly there have been inevitable changes, some maybe for the better, such as the introduction of main service amenities, but other changes, the closure of the railway for instance, are both sad and questionable.

Private enterprise has seen many changes, from the days of the horseshoe nail-maker, to the arrival of motor transport and the garage technician. The demand for cloth and wool, the cloth traders were particularly important, meant they thrived in the seventeenth and eighteenth centuries. This was when the Bourchier Family grew to prominence in Bampton.

From medieval times onwards the produce of the tanner and harness-makers was also in great demand, and present day residents speak of finding scraps of leather under floors which are being replaced or moved.

Bampton church was built in stone from local quarries, and today evidence of several quarries can be found. One such lies behind the Exeter Inn and was in use before the church was built, while Luttrell Quarry, off the Old Tiverton Road, was working during the thirteenth century when St Michael and All Angels replaced an earlier wooden building.

SCOTT'S QUARRIES

The Scott Family, led first by Archie Scott, was the last family to work commercial quarries in Bampton. Archie Scott's granddaughter, Margaret (now Hellier), and former long service employee, Donald Gould, have provided vital information and memories from which this account has been compiled. The author was delighted to receive their help as Scott's Quarries, are frequently spoken of today and remembered as being vital to Bampton's economy and way of life. The author's father, Frederick Thomas, worked for a short time in the office at Scotts in the 1960s. Early photographs around the start of the 1900s from Reg Kingdon's collection give a vivid picture of a workforce, from boss to employee, all of whom were proud of their jobs.

Sir Edwin Dunning, of Stoodleigh Court, owned Bampton and Whipcott Quarries (at Holcombe Rogus) earlier in the present century. He built New Buildings where the picturesque thatched cottages once stood beside the old cobbled road.

Workers in the Bampton stone quarry, c.1900.

An early view of the stone quarry at Bampton, taken around 1890 before the involvement of the Scott family. RK

Bampton and married into the same Burrow family, Jack Scott marrying Maud Burrow, and Agatha (Aggie) Scott marrying Victor Burrow. Archibald and Elsie Scott brought up three children, Roland (W.R.), Greta and Joan.

Jack Scott started his own haulage business in Bampton with about five small lorries, doing mostly council work. When he was unable to carry on, Archie bought his lorries.

Shortly before and during the 1914–18 war, quarrying was done mainly from Bampton and Whipcott (limestone). Hardstone was later quarried from Highleigh, Cove and Wonham. The quarry work was heavy and hard on the men and on the wonderful horses who week-in-and-week- out hauled the stone.

Around 1900 Mr. E. H. Mason, an accountant of Cheltenham, was the auditor to Bampton Quarries, and also to John White Scott of Shirenewton, near Chepstow, in Monmouthshire. J.W. Scott was a founder member of the National Traction Engine Society formed about that time and he fought a legal battle with Monmouthshire County Council for driving a steam roller along a main road. Mr. A. Scott walked in front of the roller with a red flag to make a test case, which he won with the court ruling that the road should be strong enough to take the roller!

It was lucky for Bampton that, about 1905, Mason visited Scott in Wales where he mentioned that Sir Edwin Dunning needed a clerk at Bampton. Archibald, son of J.W., applied for the job and secured it. Probably that same year Archibald was appointed manager, becoming a partner in 1913. Each partner raised £1000.

Six years later Sir Edwin Dunning sold his share to Scott for £1000, to be paid in instalments out of the profits. Archibald Scott used his father's name to register the business as J.W. Scott & Sons.

During this time Archibald met and married Miss E. Burrow of Town Mills, Bampton. Archibald's brother and sister also came to

The stone in Kersdown Quarry (on the left side going up Old Tiverton Road) was conveyed by 'drams' run on narrow-gauge lines. A steam winch and cable situated just off the Old Tiverton Road, Kersdown side, pulled the loaded drams up from the face of the quarry, over a wooden bridge (above the Old Tiverton Road), to a high spot on Ashleigh Park side, where the few trees are today. The drams then went down by gravity on to the Green (Ashleigh Park), where ponies pulled the drams across the green to a spot by Ashleigh House (although the house was not there at that time). From this point the drams (probably two or three together) travelled by gravity on a bank on the left-hand side of Tiverton Road to a point opposite the crushing plant, and there they went over the second wooden bridge. On this run a man stood on a small platform at the back of the last dram to operate a brake as it careered down and turned right over the bridge, and so to the 'cracker' as it was known. Not a job for the faint hearted!

Above: *A detail from an old Ordnance Survey map shows the extensive quarry working around Bampton, c.1900.* RK

Right: *Looking down Brook Street towards the quarry, c.1930, to where Ashleigh Park is now sited.* Photo Mrs Currie

Below: *A view from the opposite direction at the back of the old quarries, now Ashleigh Park.* Photo Mrs Currie

Two views of the Bampton stone quarries c.1900. Note the railway and the horse-drawn drams which were used to carry stone from the quarries. RK

The quarries on the right side of Old Tiverton Road (where Ashleigh Park is built) were named, from the left, Bowers Close, Pitt Hill and Bailey's Quarry.

The ponies had to pull the empty drams back to the green. A part of the line-bed can still be seen near Ashleigh House. The stables for these animals is now Hillcrest, just behind the red telephone box in Briton Street. Donald Gould lived

there for 51 years. Before that he lived at Staple Cross in a bungalow bought by Archibald Scott.

Donald recalls: 'I remember when, as a boy with Roland Scott, we both used to feed the ponies in where my house was later built.' By the early 1920s the drams were out of use and the stone was being hauled by steam lorries. The wooden bridge linking the crusher plant to the quarries was taken down in about 1930.

Block stone was the type sold to most of the Councils. Horse and cart, steam lorries, or traction engines with a trailer, hauled the stone to be deposited in road sidings. Men 'cracked' all this stone by hand, at piecework rates per cubic yard. In the sidings burnt 'lump' lime was sold. This had been produced at Bampton for many years and was sold by hogshead, usually collected from the kilns by farmers with a horses and carts.

During the same period, in the early 1920s, there was quite a substantial timber trade. The bottom yard, was known as the 'sawyard' even when the fitters' shops were built there some years later.

With the Great War causing big shortages of labour about fifteen prisoners of war, mostly Poles and Slavs were taken on. A long wooden hut was built for them in the yard. One of them became the cook and cleaner while the rest worked in the quarries and as fitters.

Before the war, and during it, stone from Whipcott was taken by barge on the canal as far as Tiverton, for which canal tolls had to be paid. Whipcott Quarry supplied all the agricultural lime for Scotts. The best limestone, from Kersdown, was worked out by the early 1900s and now contains only what is called mud stone.

Scotts had six lime kilns burning - three at Whipcott and three at Bampton. Margaret Hellier

A traction engine of J.W. Scott & Sons, on OHMS duty during the Great War at the Nook, Bampton. Jack Scott is seen standing on the far left and it was he who later sold all his vehicles to Archie Scott. RK

A brand new Sentinel steam lorry proudly displaying the livery of J.W. Scott & Son.

Members of the Scott family and their workers line up in front of the company vehicles, sometime between 1914–18. Two Ford lorries stand at each end, and the traction engines carry a certificate declaring them to be On His Majesty's Service. RK

recalled: 'When I was living at home in Ashleigh House, I would wake some nights and yell at my father, "The works are on fire!" But it was the red hot kilns glowing in the dark.'

Scotts had the first steam lorries in Bampton, made by Fodens. They also had steamrollers and nine traction engines. Later vehicles, preferred to the Fodens, were Sentinels. These were slow and solid vehicles, driven on solid tyres, with a speed restriction of 12mph (average fuel consumption 18 miles per cwt.).

In 1924 W.R. Scott left school to go to the Sentinel Wagon Works at Shrewsbury for a two-year engineering course. Road rolling and tar spraying were a substantial part of the business at this time and it was in about 1920 when the first streets in Bampton were tar sprayed, by Scotts, naturally. Prior to this the road metal on the streets was just water-bound; mud in winter and clouds of dust in the summer. The Council, or Scotts, had to go round the streets with a water cart twice a day, damping down in dry weather!

Scotts now had several steamrollers, water carts, gritters and tar sprayers. Annual contracts for tar-spraying were obtained from Taunton District Council as well as the local councils. A depot was opened in Wood Street, Taunton, where there was garaging for several lorries, living vans and other plant. The men remained in Taunton for the week returning to Bampton at weekends.

Surface-dressing chipping was dispatched from Bampton siding to Taunton station and off-loaded into lorries by the driver (and his stoker) using

This Sentinel lorry has double back wheels, each with solid rubber tyres. It also bears the company phone number, Bampton 6. Photo A. Dixon

only hand shovels. There were no mechanical loaders, in those days.

Scotts built the Bampton reservoir about 1925–26. Previously the Bampton supply came directly from the springs near the Primary School. Later the water was pumped up to the Bampton reservoir off High Street. New water mains were laid through the town by Frank Lazarus who later set up his own building firm in Tiverton. All this excavation was done by hand: pick, shovel and wheelbarrow!

About 1925 Scotts bought the first Fowler-Wood machine in the South West. This was a steamroller built by John Fowler of Leeds. It had two sweepers in the front which were geared to

Above and right: *Scott workers building a reservoir at Brighton in 1934. The men in the photo, right, are l-r: Frank 'Nibby', Staddon; Bill Taylor, (five unknown); George Herniman; Bill (Bob?) Rowland; Jack Ware; George Hutter; Harold Rowland; Archie Scott. The excavator driver is Walt Gould.* RK

the roller, to clear the roadway. Hot tar stored in a tank at the back of the roller was sprayed under pressure to the road, and a gritter towed behind laid the surface chippings. When the tar tank was empty the roller returned to the starting point to refill from the tar boiler, rolling in the surface chippings on the way. Miles and miles of country roads were surfaced with this machine.

Wages were: labourer 8d per hour £1.6s 0d per week; quarryman and driver 9d per hour; foreman and fitter 10d per hour; carpenter and blacksmith 1 shilling per hour; hire of horse and cart 6 shillings per day. There were no annual holidays but there were six paid public holidays. The only

deduction from pay was 4d to 9d per week National Insurance. The average price of stone was 4 shillings a ton for block and 7 shillings a ton for chippings. These prices and rates of pay hardly varied from before 1920 to the mid 1930s.

At this time two Ruston excavators were purchased. As a proven, reliable business Scotts were given big contracts far away from Bampton, and the chance to use these new machines. The Exeter by-pass was one job, and the workforce had to travel to Brighton to excavate a reservoir where a fleet of Sentinels were employed to haul away.

Mr. J. C. Bent (owner of Westleigh Stone & Lime Co.) purchased land at Rockbeare and engaged Scotts excavators to open up a gravel pit, now EEC Quarries, Rockbeare.

When the 1934 Transport Act became law it was decided to have a separate transport organisation. In this way the vehicles would have 'A' licences with no limitations in their operation. So, all the quarrying and contracting interests were transferred to a new limited liability company, Scotts (Bampton) Ltd, with A. Scott and W. R. Scott as directors. J. W. Scott & Sons was, from 1934, a transport firm owned by A. Scott.

During the 1939–45 war the company took part in the supply of materials for the construction of aerodromes at Chivenor, Exeter and Dunkeswell.

To encourage food production, the Ministry of Agriculture gave a large grant for the installation of new lime-grinding equipment at Higher Whipcott for the production of carbonate of lime, used as a fertiliser. To this end, for many years after, a large part of the lime requirement was supplied by Scotts (Scotts Magnesium Lime).

Meanwhile, the contracting side had been extended. Men were employed in the London area, repairing war damaged buildings. Various properties owned by A. Scott were reconstructed and kept in repair by the building workforce, and the stables in Briton Street were converted into a house, Hillcrest. The workforce now stood at 130.

Excluding fixed plant and equipment there were: 35 lorries, 5 lime spreaders, 10 landrovers, vans and cars, 6 loaders and 4 excavators.

In 1951 Mr Mason ceased as the company's accountant after 50 years service. In 1956 the company purchased Highleigh Quarry from Mrs Somerset. The quarry was previously let on a Royalty basis.

In 1955 Archie Scott purchased Hamslade and Stuckeridge properties from the executors of Miss MacAllister. Planning permission to extract minerals from part of Stuckeridge was obtained and stone was later extracted, mainly for Clatworthy reservoir. These properties were leased to the company by M. Scott and were incorporated into the forestry, game and poultry rearing side of the business. Gamekeepers were employed at these sites and a shooting syndicate formed.

In 1957 the Company obtained the contract to supply all the hardstone requirements to build Clatworthy Dam. Hardstone had to be used as limestone was too soft. About 120 000 tons of stone, mostly from Highleigh, were crushed at Bampton works and it was all delivered to Clatworthy in Scotts' own transport. A new crushing plant and some washing equipment (for stone) were installed for this job.

In 1953, the Directors of Scotts invited all their employees to a dinner and presentation for service at Clapps, Tiverton. The photograph was taken at the company works before leaving in hired buses. RK

A presentation for long service at Scotts, 1968. l-r: William Taylor (53 years' service)' Donald Gould (Secretary); Roland Scott (Managing Director); James Yeo (45 years' service). RK

Between 1974–76 Scotts hauled alternate days with Cove Quarries (Holmingham) in the construction of Wimbleball reservoir. Over 200 000 tons of hardstone were supplied and, throughout this period, Devon and Somerset Councils were still being provided with their local needs. Also the supply of agricultural lime, burnt lime and carbonate of lime continued.

In 1959, when the Clatworthy reservoir contract was coming to an end, Archibald Scott died. W. R. Scott (Roland) then became the proprietor of J.W. Scott & Sons, and chairman of the company, with Mrs E. Scott, Mrs E. E. Scott and Mrs M.A. Hellier as directors.

Cove Quarry was later sold to Major North as a Nature Reserve, and Highleigh Quarry was sold as another Nature Reserve to Mr Cooling.

By 1966 the government lime subsidy had been so reduced that the farmer was paying double the amount of a few years earlier. In consequence sales fell considerably and Whipcott became uneconomic. In December 1966, Whipcott Quarry plant and various mineral rights nearby were sold to EEC Quarries, and the quarries at Bampton, for the first time in a century or more of business, ceased to be in the lime trade. In 1972, due to the reduced number of lorries being operated by J.W. Scott & Sons, Roland Scott decided to transfer his interests to the company. So ended the name J.W. Scott & Sons, originally formed in 1919. This brought to a close an important era in the history of Bampton. Locally quarried stone is most attractive and was used widely in local buildings, where it will continue to be a constant reminder of quarrying days in Bampton.

As a major employer the Scott family was well respected in Bampton. As Margaret Hellier recalled: 'At the height of business we employed 130 people. I worked from time to time in the office and it took me two days to make up the weekly wage packets'.

On Bampton Fair Day, Mrs Archie Scott used to invite all their clients to a big luncheon, whereupon the clients usually returned the compliment by settling their accounts!

Scotts first fleet of short-wheelbased lorries were a familiar sight, chugging the narrow lanes and roads with the well known dark blue colour and yellow and red lettering. Although heavily loaded, the drivers were always courteous to horse riders. How some of the modern goods vehicle drivers today could learn from them!

On 9 July 1996 Scotts ceased trading and Camas became the owners of Kersdown Quarry. At the time of writing the 'cracker' or stone-crusher and supporting buildings, weighbridge and offices, are in the throes of demolition at the southern approach of the town. No more grey

Left: *Wimbleball Lake was built with the help of stone quarried at Bampton. The dam and reservoir nestle in the valley of the River Haddeo on the edge of Exmoor.* Author

Right: *All that's left of the 'cracker' at Bampton quarry which is now a derelcit site. There is a hope that a new community centre may be built on the site, funds permitting.* BS

dust clouds belching above the 'cracker' as it ground and crunched in full throttle.

The one reminder of the stone quarry is Ashleigh House, built by the Scott family, standing in a prominent position a few yards from the now silent works yard. Arnold Seward, in the notes he wrote of his memories, included this song which he says was sung at Scotts:

Way down in cracker yard
Thats where they work so hard,
They work there night and day
And hardly get no pay
When they wake up in the morning,
They can here old Archie calling,
Get out of bed, you —
Get out of bed, you —
And get down to the cracker yard!.

OTHER BUSINESSES

The 1850 *Gazetteer and Directory of Devonshire*. loaned to the author by Bill Hancock of Church Terrace, lists over a hundred names of Bampton people, from Clergy to Carriers, Innkeepers to Doctors. This number does not include the many farmers in the parish. Other people, including Olive and Bill Hampton of Castle Street, and Revd Tony Grosse, who is retired and lives in Frog Street, have also provided old documents. All prove how Bampton has been a go-ahead and industrious community since records began. Strangely enough Bampton has the closure of the railway to thank for the present main employers whose businesses now occupy the old railway goods yard.

THE SEWARD FAMILY BAKERY

Seward's is one of two Bampton bakeries producing traditional bread, the other being Frank Bawden in Brook Street. Len Sampson who bakes the bread these days grew up with Brian Seward, in Bampton. There was a third bakery at the top of Brook Street a few years ago, formerly Escotts, so Bamptonians have been more than lucky when needing fresh bread. This business has a personal interest to the author and warrants a place in the book if only for the length of time it has remained in continuous trading - ninety years - offering a reliable service in a small community, and still going strong!

Where Hair Care is owned and run by Rosemary Totterdell at the bottom of Mary Lane in Brook Street, the two Coren sisters sold materials and cotton, and tins of biscuits. One sister was unmarried, the other was a Mrs Watts. Longer ago the Post Office was sited here.

Rex Serenger's hardware store and petrol pumps in Fore Street is another long-established business, having been started before the Sewards but in another name, Butler, that of his grandfather on his mother's side. The store has for many years been a postcard picture, with its attractive layout of stock and its colourful flower-fronted facade on the road junction.

Rex and his wife, Doreen, were familiar faces in everyday Bampton life in their store until Doreen died tragically young. She was one of those extra-special people who everyone loved, and she in return was never heard to say a bad word about anyone. She loved arranging the china and pots and pans in different displays, meticulously dusted. They both supported local events and

Bampton people will always remember Doreen for her bright, bubbly personality and kind nature.

Ern, Rex's father, used to work for John Seward doing deliveries by horse and cart. Then Rex began his own business at No. 1 High Street, selling wallpaper and paint. He had trained to be a builder and has always taken a pride in retaining the old character of buildings during subsequent building jobs. At one time both Rex and Ern were on the town council together. Ern liked a change, owning the Bridge House Hotel and The Wishing Well at various times.

Serenger's store was the first in Bampton to have petrol pumps installed, in 1925. Prior to that time petrol could be bought in two gallon cans. For a time there were also petrol pumps on the forecourt of Kings in Back Street. Once owned by Gerald Burnett the well known electrician.

An unusual item fixed above Rex's shop door is a man trap, that came from Bittescombe Manor in 1890.

Bampton Pharmacy, next door to Serenger's, was the Angel Inn, mentioned earlier, and seen in

BAMPTON IN BUSINESS

Sammy Gibbings' Temperance Hotel c.1900. In more recent years this became The Bridge House Hotel. RK

George Davey, wheelwright and blacksmith, stands outside his premises in Back Street, c.1910. RK

BAMPTON IN BUSINESS

Above: Shops and shoppers, delivery boys and tradesmen pose for the camera in Fore Street, c.1910. On the left is Escott's, baker and confectioner, and further up the Street is Staddon's, upholsterers. The posters on the wall advertise, among other things, The Royal Agricultural Show, and Keating's Powders. RK

F. C. DAVEY,
Saddler, Harness and Collar Maker,
BAMPTON.

Whips, Spurs, Bridles, and every article in the line on the Lowest Terms.

Trunks, Portmanteaus and Suit Cases Sold and Repaired.

Waterproof Aprons, Mackintoshes, Leggings, Brushes, Sponges, Tarpaulins' etc.

Agent for Devon & Exeter Savings Bank

Above and right: *The Davey family were involved in saddlery and blacksmithing. The Davey premises in Fore Street is now Crispin House.* RK

BAMPTON IN BUSINESS

George Davey, wheelwright, carpenter and blacksmith, based at Back Street. This photograph, c.1910, reveals the trend towards the demise of horsepower in favour of the petrol engine: the BP Union Flag sign on the gate, the cans of motor spirit standing outside the shop, and the window posters advertising Lister petrol and oil engines. RK

Right: An earlier view of Davey's premises, taken c.1900. The window advertisements are for 'Davey's Cycles - Fitted With Bowden Brakes' and the yard is full of agricultural and industrial equipment. RK

George Davey and Sons' works were around the Nook, Silver Street. Here they display their agricultural equipment. A photograph thought to be taken around Fair Day c.1900. RK

BAMPTON IN BUSINESS

Above: *Seward's Bakery, 1910. Here John Seward is seen holding the horse, while Nina Seward stands in the doorway and Tom Seward (a brother) stands on the left. In the bread cart is Jimmy Fisher.* BS

Right: *Town Mills c.1890. The mills were owned by the Burrow family, and a mill on this site is mentioned in the Domesday Book.* RK

Vicary's butcher's shop in Newton Square, c.1900.

BAMPTON IN BUSINESS

A splendid photograph of workmen on the scaffolding of New Buildings c.1900. These were built by Sir Edwin Dunning of Scott's Quarries. RK

Podbery's shop, now the Spar Shop, remains almost unscathed following the arson attack in 1905 which resulted in an explosion completely destroying one building and damaging others. The castle mound can be seen in the background. RK

BAMPTON IN BUSINESS

Staddon's Temperance Hotel around 1910, Note the Red Lion adjoining in Back Street. Note also the petrol pump standing at the corner of the building. RK

Below: Two views of the Druggists Arms in Fore Street, one c.1895 (proprietor H. Tate), when the road was still unmetalled, and the other c.1910 when it sported its own petrol pump and motor garage opening on to a tarmac road. RK

a number of the photos. The Constitutional Club was held here and there was a very large, long room upstairs used for billiards.

Keith and Jenny Frost run the Pharmacy today, and going back several years we find Gilbert Todd and his wife Emily running it for fifty years. Some of the old bottles, containing strange-sounding ingredients, Keith still keeps, the empty bottles being attractive decorations, as well as a part of local history.

Mr Butler owned both ends of the 'island' in Fore Street and really would have liked to own it all. However when 'Toddy' died, Emily Todd wanted Rex to buy the chemist premises, which he did. Nowadays Rex owns the whole island.

On the opposite side of Fore Street is John Record's garage. John's interest lies in old cars and often one, lovingly restored and polished, stands inside the window.

These premises and the house next door were once the Druggist's Arms and the Commercial Hotel. It was originally H. Langdon's Chemist, Grocer & Stationer, Wine & Spirit Merchant and Genuine Patent Cattle Medicines, and sold draught Sherry at l/6d per bottle, along with other supplies. A contemporary advertisement also boasts that the place was an 'Agent for Sun Fire and Life and Railway Passengers' Accidental Insurance Association.'

John once found an old quart bottle with stopper top, possibly a beer bottle, on which was

BAMPTON IN BUSINESS

The Exter Inn, c.1920. Photo Mrs Currie

Below: *Newton Square c. 1910. Note Gare's the chemist, the building facing on the left, with the community tap, centre, and the oil street lamp. On the right, by the figures, is the Wheelwrights Inn.* Photo Mrs Currie

BAMPTON IN BUSINESS

Turner's in Castle Street, c.1910. Note the impressive cement facade. There is an ornate baclony, a private entrance separate to the shop doorway, and cattle in the street! Photo Mrs Currie

Below: The Railway Temperance Hotel in Luke Street, c.1940. Vicary's butcher's shop can be seen at the foot of the hill. RK

Bottom: *Mr Vicary stands outside his shop in Newton Square, in the late 1930s.* RK

BAMPTON IN BUSINESS

The Black Cat Cafe and garage, Stuckeridge Bridge, late 1940s. All photos Mrs Currie

Below: *F.T. Seward, Coal, Coke and Forage Merchant, c.1900*

Bottom: *Fore Street, with the White Horse Hotel and petrol pumps on the right, c.1950.*

written 'Henry Tate, Bampton'. The stopper may not be the original as it reads, Hancock, Wiveliscombe 1926.

Jack Gillard remembers: 'Next to John Record's garage on the corner of Castle and Fore Street used to be Mr and Mrs Atkins' Haberdashery shop, selling anything from reels of cotton to shoe-laces and sweets. For some reason Mr Atkins was nicknamed 'Quacky' and the corner was locally referred to as Quacky's corner.'

Mr Atkins used to go by train to outlying places with two baskets full of his wares. Present members of the family heard about this book and were delighted to find their grandfather is in the the photograph of the 1887 Jubilee celebrations.

'Siddy Wood, who lived with the Atkins, travelled to all the markets and sheep auctions, such as Anstey and Molland, selling from his baskets.' Jack recalled.

Of course the narrow Back Street ran behind the Angel, as we see in a photograph of the Lion, where Cis Croucher lives. Later, part of her house was the Gospel Hall and Central Hall, when it was part of Staddon's Corner House, a Temperance Hotel (which served no alcohol). There used to be some sort of fuel pump by the front door.

Going further up Back Street we find George Davey & Son, who were wheelwrights and blacksmiths.

BAMPTON IN BUSINESS

WILLIAM NOTT & SONS

Jack Parkhouse

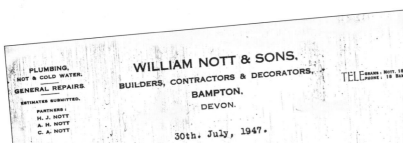

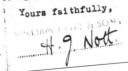

Wally Hancock

Jack Mogridge

Photos of workers from the firm of Nott & Sons, one of Bampton's best known companys. Above is a letter from the firm, dated 1947, appointing Derek Aldridge as an apprentice-carpenter at sixpence per hour.

BAMPTON IN BUSINESS

WILLIAM NOTT & SONS

Left l-r: *Wally Hancock, Jack Mogridge, Jack Parkhouse, Ken Coles.*

Right l-r: *Bernard How, Derek Aldridge, E Waite.*

Derek Aldridge, now retired, is seen in 1998 at work on the new figure for the White Horse Inn. Inside the carving is placed a book about local people, along with memorabilia from Bampton.
Information and photos provided by Derek Aldridge

BAMPTON IN BUSINESS

The White Horse tap (cider bar), Fore Street, c. 1900. RK

A view down Fore Street, c.1900. The White Horse stands on the left, the Angel Inn on the right. RK

BAMPTON IN BUSINESS

The Exter Inn, c.1910. RK

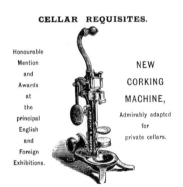

CELLAR REQUISITES.

Honourable
Mention
and
Awards
at
the
principal
English
and
Foreign
Exhibitions.

NEW
CORKING
MACHINE,

Admirably adapted
for
private cellars.

The Castle Inn, Castle Street, in the early years of the twentieth century when the landlord was William Kingdom. RK

BAMPTON IN BUSINESS

Right: *Harry Sampson, the undertaker, outside his premises in Frog Street, now the home of Joy Coles, her daughter.* Photo Diana Thomas

Far right: *Inside the Swan 1959. John Fayter who, in the 1960s, used to sell logs.* Author

Below: *Fred Edworthy, railway worker, postman, and fish and chip shop owner, with Ern Kerslake and Diana Severn (with dog) talking to 'Tom' Thomas in the Swan, 1959 (the author's father was landlord)* Author

Above left: *Brian Seward taking a customer's Christmas dinner out of the bakery ovens.* Middle right above: *Outside the fish and chip shop.* Above right: *The old chemist's shop of Mr Todd being decorated in May 1968 by Rex Serenger.*

Newton Square was an open-air market area for animals, usually sheep on the old Fair Day. The Swan Hotel, like Costcutters today, was only two storeys high for many years. It was after the coming of the railway that the Swan had the top floor built on, to accommodate the extra trade.

Along Station Road the three-storey former warehouse is now owned by Rick Ditton, who is turning it into a flat. It once was a grain warehouse and the sacks were hauled up to the top floor by a chain and pulley. Later Hookins Oil, which was founded by Bert Hookins, with him in charge,

An old photograph of a trade stand incorporated into a recent advertisement for Hookins, one of Bampton most successful companies.

used this store for motor and engine oil, again using the chain and pulley. Hookins Oils flourished, so needing more room they moved into Lords Meadow, just a stones-throw away, off West Street. Bert was joined by Stewart, his son, and now Bert's grandson, Graham, has joined the business. Stewart's wife, Penny, looks after the office. Their business has gone on for over 50 years too!

The fondly remembered Goods Yard at Bampton Station has changed with the times and become a modern small Industrial Esate. Rotolok, an engineering firm owned by entrepreneur-businessman, Dan McCauley, was established here in the mid 1970s, a decade or so after the the railway closed.

Global Chemicals offers out work as well as line work within the factory to many locals today. Recently they have expanded on to another site at Exebridge Industrial Estate.

Origins, has a reputation for up-market ladies' wear, using a wide range of Liberty print fabrics among their range. They draw customers from a wide area.

Standing just off the original railway bridge and beside the former station master's house, in Luke Street, is the Bridge House Hotel, also a former Temperance house. Sammy Gibbings, the Town Crier, lived here, selling sweets, while his wife catered for cyclists.

Today Brian Smith assures his guests of a warm welcome. He caters for fishermen during the summer and sporting parties for shooting and horse-racing in the winter. Brian and his wife Val. who was Irish, often had Irish folk-music playing in the bar. Val was a wonderful girl and tremendously brave when she accepted the chance of a double lung transplant to try and improve her quality of life. For almost a year she conquered many post operative problems and always smiled and kept optimistic. It was a great shock to everyone who loved her when the final battle could not be won.

Sustrans today are creating new routes for cyclists throughout the South West, with 'stamping stations' along the way for their route cards. Seward store is the station in Bampton, thus continuing a tradition of catering for cyclists by such as Staddons Corner House, and Sammy Gibbings shop.

BAMPTON IN BUSINESS

DELIVERING THE GOODS - 1960S

Top left: *Mr Napper outside Miss Besley's Dairy, c.1967. WI*

Top centre: *Mr Hollick delivering milk in South Street for Mr Southwood. WI*

Top right: *Mr Cleverley on his newspaper round. WI*

Centre left: *The daily milk delivery from Exeter. WI*

Centre right: *Sercombe's fruit and veg lorry outside Morris' shop. WI*

Fred Moore receiving the Imperial Services Medal for 25 years' service with the Post Office. l-r: Chris Rendell; Ted Ford; Parsons; Fred Moore; Alf Berry; Mr Bittiscombe, Stan Quick; Madge Gullidge. RK

Castle Street around 1910. Note the cart loaded with tree bark for use in the tanneries at the Old House in Frog Street. RK

Along Frog Street was the Tannery or Tan Yard as locals still call it, beside the Old House. A photograph shows a horse-drawn cart loaded ready for the Tan Yard.

We now move into Brook Street, which Bampton residents have used for all kinds of celebrations and marches. From Newton Square down into Briton Street, at the south end of Brook Street, there are many photographs which show what a bustling and happy place Bampton always has been.

Businesses sit close to each other in Brook Street offering everything from food supplies, financial services, flowers, postal services, banking, (but only on two mornings a week), and hair dressing. The type of shops and trades have changed with demand. No longer can you buy horse-shoe nails,

and what was the laundry is now a private house, once lived in by Michael and Chris Rendell.

When the sheep trade died leatherwork expanded. Around the 1850s eight shoemakers are known: five Escotts, two Oxenhams and a James Surridge. Much earlier than this John Webber was a well-known sergemaker in Bampton. He died in 1764 and his two daughters are featured elsewhere in this book.

Another successful business was established by Julie Cridland in 1996. Whilst grooming her own dog, Julie wondered if other pet owners might like her to groom their dogs, and so she set up Diamond Dogs Grooming service, quickly establishing a regular clientele within about a fifteen mile radius of Bampton.

Bampton railway station in the 1920s. RK

Chapter 6 - The Railway

One of the saddest moments in the history of Bampton was the day Dr Beeching decided to close the railway. Despite all good reasoning otherwise, 5 October 1963 was the last day a delightful steam train (and one diesel train) chugged in and out of Bampton station.

The station setting was picturesque, like a theatre stage surrounded by a high gallery for an appreciative audience. All the land around was higher than the railway so when you looked down on the neat and clean station it was almost as if the trains were giant toys. Many an hour has been whiled away on the bridge waiting for the 'up' train to engulf you in steam as it chuffed its way on towards Morebath.

Bampton railway station opened in 1884, creating the chance for everyone to travel one of the most beautiful areas in Devon: the Exe Valley. The river Exe rises high on Exmoor at Exehead, on one side of a hill. On the other side of that same hill the river Barle rises. These two rivers meander in the same direction through scenic Exmoor country creating many leisure opportunities for salmon fishing, walking, canoeing, and horse riding. Eventually the rivers meet at Exebridge, a village two miles north of Bampton, and continue as the River Exe, flowing downstream along the western Bampton parish boundary until it meets the river Batherm, then flowing south out of Bampton beside the railway track. The rivers meet near where the black iron railway bridge crosses the Exe at Holmingham Farm.

Many Bamptonians feel that if Dr Beeching had foreseen the over-crowded roads, shortage of car parks, air pollution from vehicles, infrequent bus services, especially for school children in bad weather, and the surge of tourism, maybe he would not have wielded his axe on Bampton Station.

With the popularity of steam trains rewarding those people who resurrected the West Somerset Railway and the Dart Valley Railway for thousands of tourists to enjoy, Bampton must surely have been worth saving too. Imagine how popular a round trip along the Exe Valley from Tiverton to Bampton would be for visitors. An opportunity to look at the wonderful flower displays throughout the town and back to Tiverton after a cream tea, would be a major attraction. Surely a missed opportunity.

One of the earliest views showing the railway, looking down Frog Street from Birchdown Cleeves, c.1910. RK

Railway Days

Three views of Bampton railway and station, taken in the early decades of the twentieth century. Top: A view over the station and goods yard c.1910. Centre: A goods train draws into the station and empty platform, c.1930.
Bottom: A photo taken from the road bridge showing the sidings, and goods shed in the distance, 1920s.
all photos RK

Railway Days

Left: *A remarkable picture of the goods shed under construction, before the line was built. The gentleman in the hat holds two dogs still for the photograph. On the left can just be seen a set of sheerlegs used to left heavy weights.* RK

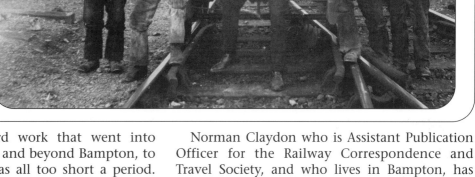

Right: *Bampton railwaymen, taken around 1900. L-r: Jim Milton (Albert Gratton's grandfather); Bill Gadd (Mrs Brice's father); Mr White; Jim Hancock (Bill Hancock's father); Alfred Saffin (ganger).* RK

Considering the hard work that went into getting the railway into and beyond Bampton, to run a mere 79 years was all too short a period. And it was not only people who travelled; Exmoor ponies could be sent by train to be sold at Bampton Fair, and then transported on from Bampton to work in the Welsh coal pits. Old photographs show them being herded towards the station.

Other freight sent by rail were the many tons of building stone from the quarries at Bampton. Around six lime kilns, owned by Scotts, produced large quantities of lime for agricultural use, much of it transhipped elsewhere by rail. As described earlier, narrow-gauge tramways connected the stone quarries with the sidings where small wagons were gravity-fed to the goods yard, returning drawn by horses.

Norman Claydon who is Assistant Publication Officer for the Railway Correspondence and Travel Society, and who lives in Bampton, has kindly written about the types of locomotives which used our line.

The locomotives most associated with the Bampton trains are the little Collett 0.4.2T's built between 1932–36, a total of 75 engines, all built at Swindon. There were always a number of them in the West Country, with quite a few at Exeter depot, for use on branch line services. Originally numbered 4800-74, they were renumbered 1400-74 in 1946 and withdrawal commenced in 1956.

These engines were auto-fitted, that is they could be used on push–pull services, and two Exeter engines were usually kept at Tiverton Junction for services to Tiverton and Hemyock.

Railway Days

A crowded platform at Bampton station, taken some time before the First World War, The photo was possibly taken on Bampton Fair Day, hence the crowd, who are heading home to Exmoor. RK

A guard checks the door of a third class carriage as a train waits to pull away from the station, around 1910. On the far platform is a neat garden, complete with pond and statuette, with a greenhouse backing on to the building housing the Gentlemen's toilet. RK

Railway Days

A train entering Bampton station around 1910. Inset: A Bampton to West Exe (Tiverton) Workman's Return ticket from 1944. RK

Four of the class are preserved, operating at Didcot, on the Dart Valley line, and of course No. 1442 is in Tiverton Museum.

Also used on the line for freight and occasional passenger services were members of the standard 'Pannier' o.6.OT, of which over 700 were built for service all over the G.W.R. It is possible that the larger 45xx 2.6.2T might also have put in an occasional appearance. These engines were operated over the larger branch lines and one of them can now be seen working from time to time on the West Somerset or Dart Valley lines.

At the end, before the Bampton service ceased, Exeter depot had five members of the Collett class on it's books, these being Nos. 1440/51/62/68/71, and these would have worked the last trains.

Since 1963 a modern industrial estate has sprung up on the remaining goods yard at Bampton. At one time four trains ran in each direction daily, connecting Morebath with Tiverton, via Bampton. In pre-war days about 60 local people used the trains each day, this number rising after the Second World War up to 200, together with general freight. The whole experience of travelling by this delightful 'Puffing Billy' as it meandered through lush meadows long before tractors and machinery replaced the farmer and his horses was relaxing and pleasant. Ladies never feared to be alone in a train compartment.

The train passed through wonderful woodlands where the first delicate bright green sprigs of larch trees heralded the start of spring, and gorse bushes, dotted with early golden flowers, blossomed in the railway cuttings.

For those who wished to go north, the train disappeared in a spectacular cloud of white steam beneath the stone railway bridge where the traffic enters downhill from High Street into the one way slip road, by the Bridge House Hotel.

The old railway bridge wall can still be seen at the back of the flower beds on the island between the hotel and the car park. When standing there, spare a thought for all the railway life of years past, lying buried beneath your feet. You can see how sharp the bend was on to the bridge from South Molton, before the road was widened after the line closed.

Once past the bridge the train chugged through the meadows and woods of the river Shuttern valley to Lodfin level crossing before bearing left-handed into Morebath Junction. On again, still bearing left, it crossed the Tiverton-to-Minehead road at Exebridge, passing over the River Exe prior to Dulverton Station. The name of this stop seemed a little misleading as the station was in the village of Brushford some two miles short of Dulverton. The Carnarvon Arms Hotel has retained the station buildings which are now converted into living accommodation.

Railway Days

Bampton railway packers (maintenance), around 1910. L-r: Alfie Saffin; Bob Murray; unknown; Bobby Alderman; unknown. RK

A train at the platform, around 1930. RK

While many railway bridges have been demolished, you still drive carefully over the narrow angled one at Brushford as you head by road to Dulverton. It was then possible to travel by train either to Barnstaple in North Devon along a pleasant valley, or to catch a train going eastwards to Taunton.

Trains were usually on time and those people who lived close enough to Bampton station found they listened for the familiar 'chuff, chuff, chuff' at the appropriate time of day, just as the chimes of the nearby parish church clock punctuated their day. Children loved to disappear for a few seconds in the cloud of 'smoke' either side of the bridge.

It was an emotional moment to see the familiar, tall fir trees being felled after the line closure. Either side of the station for many a long year they had lined the high banks, their dark evergreen foliage rippling in the wind. It was hard for locals to accept that neither the trees, nor the familiar sight of a friendly steam engine, would ever be seen in Bampton again. However time moves on and now covering the station site is a large car park, much needed to sustain the ever-increasing volume of motor transport.

The queues of heavy summer holiday traffic and freight for North Devon along the old A361 have been alleviated by the construction of the North Devon Link Road (the new A 361), south of Bampton. Today visitors to Bampton can park easily, few ever realising that a once-busy railway station lies beneath them.

Bampton is a prominent competitor in the Britain in Bloom competition, as it has been for almost thirty years. This draws many visitors to enjoy the spectacularly colourful hanging baskets and flower displays throughout the streets and in every nook and cranny, all summer. Bampton station would have helped that cause tremendously as it had bright and cheerful flower beds, carefully tended by Cyril Kennard and then by Wilf Jefferies. A photograph taken in 1910 shows that even a greenhouse stood on the south side of the waiting room complex. There was a fish pond too, complete with goldfish.

Railway Days

Locomotive 1471 being boarded at Bampton c.1950. Note the West Street entrance on the right, over the track from the Luke Street entrance. Mid Devon Gazette

Railway Days

MOREBATH

Morebath Junction Halt opened on 1 December 1928 and on the platform was built a small shelter to protect passengers from the vagaries of the Exmoor weather. The Halt was a quarter of a mile away from the village itself, without a proper road, or even a footpath between, just a track!

Above: *Morebath Junction and Morebath Halt, c.1930.* RK

Left: *Morebath Station, 1920.* RK

Below: *Morebath junction and signal box, 1963. The signalman stands at the trackside with the key which allows the train to pass safely on to the next station.* RK

The low-lying position of the station meant a walk downhill from either entrance. From the Swan Hotel side the entrance was wide enough for vehicles to get to the station buildings. Horses and carts in the early days, later motor vehicles. The second entrance was at the top of the bridge, sloping down the West Street bank, only accessible for pedestrians. A return ticket from Bampton to Tiverton in 1959 was nine-pence-halfpenny, about 4 pence in today's money!

Bampton Town Band led by Neddy Northcott turned out to play for the very last train. Locals packed the station but alas the author could not join them, as her eldest son, Roger, had arrived into the world the previous day. He had travelled many times on the train he never saw!

Railway Days

Above: *Locals come to see the last train out of Bampton Station, October 1963. Among them are members of the Town Band and Alec Hancock, Marjory Vodden, Diana Thomas, Albert and Mrs Curtis.* RK

Left: *A bulldozer fills in the old trackway to make the new road across the railway station, 1964.* RK

The Bampton YFC show and sale at Bampton market , early 1950s. Main competitors l-r: Kath Holloway; May Palfrey; Alan Rowland. Judges l-r: Herbert Gibbons and Amos Bridgeman. Photo A. Rowland

Chapter 7 - Farming Families

With the BSE crisis currently preying upon the minds of all farmers, looking through the scrap books of Bampton Women's Institute and from Eileen Shere, the disease all farmers once feared, was foot-and-mouth. This had broken out in 1967–68 locally causing great distress in the farming community and even disrupting social life. Prior to this time the disease had been in our area in the 1940s.

Livestock prices have seldom been lower in modern times, although prices have fluctuated greatly with demand over the years. A report from Bampton fatstock market in May 1972 records the Champion Young Farmers steer from W. Weston of Kersdown Barton, weighed just over half a ton, and was sold for £16 per cwt.

Where farming dominates the way of life in any area, the children are frequently encouraged to belong to their local Young Farmers Club. Bampton has had a strong membership over the years, with members participating in all kinds of farming-related competitions, often coming out on top. Competitions cover every aspect of farm life, from animal husbandry to skill with machinery - on the domestic side covering dairy work and cookery. In 1972 we find local restauranteur Edward Tanner as one of the Club Leaders, with William Weston, of Kersdown Barton, the Chairman. Eileen Shere was Assistant Secretary, and the Advisory Committee included Alan Rowland, of Wick Farm, A. Holloway of Zeal Farm, and S Kelland of Pipshayne.

Zeal Farm stands above Shillingford and is the home of the Holloway family today but two photographs they recently received show the family who lived at Zeal until around 1930. Mrs. Janet Holloway kindly offered them for this book. Zeal also had a small Chapel in earlier times, although it would appear not to have been dedicated.

Left: *Enjoying open-topped motoring at Zeal Farm in the 1930s.* Photo Janet Holloway

Right: *Zeal Farm 1908. Dennis Goddard's grandfather, Thomas, on horse; grandmother Ann Pring (née Baker) on left; her sister Florrie (right), with Dennis' father (with dog) and brother Albert.* Photo Janet Holloway

Herb and Hettie Gamlin's wedding at Dipford Farm c.1909. Back row l-r: Mrs Mantle (grandmother); Mr Mantle (granfather); others unknown; Front row l-r: Herbert Webber; Mr F. Webber; Mrs F. Webber; Kathleen Webber; Mr S. Webber (grandfather); bridesmaid (unknown); H. Gamlin (groom); Hettie Webber (bride); Lily Webber (bridesmaid); Emily Webber (grandmother); unknown; Frank Webber; child unknown.

Sally Luxton of Parsonage Farm, Petton, was looking through her scrap books and found the following photographs of her husband, John's family who lived and farmed at Shillingford and Petton.

John Luxton and Brian Seward, are cousins, sharing Fred Webber as their grandfather. Fred farmed with his wife May at Dipford Farm, Shillingford, where John's mother Kathy and Brian's mother, Dorrie, grew up. Fred moved into Dipford when his parents, who had farmed there some time, moved out. They went to Sunderleigh Farm, close by.

'Granfer', as we younger ones knew Fred, was a great character whose life revolved around hunting. He taught the author to drive a car out hunting! Long before there was transport to take the horses to the meet, Fred would get up in the morning and ride to Dunkery Hill Gate or Brendon Two Gates out on Exmoor, sometimes twenty miles. The same horse would hunt all day

and then be ridden home, often walking through Bampton as midnight struck on the church clock. These animals were well fed and cared for and loved their 'boss' and would probably gallop any present-day horse off its legs.

Most farms had an orchard. Fred made his own scrumpy cider, as many farmers did. It was powerful stuff, quite unlike the refined bottled products of today! Drunk in excessive quantities it was either mind-blowing or a powerful laxative, sometimes both!

Dorrie and Kathy used to ride their pony into Bampton to go to school, and later they rode bikes in to catch the train to Tiverton for their senior school days. The pony, or bikes, were left at the Castle Hotel.

Another branch of the family lived in Castle House, opposite the hotel. This house is now divided into two, and the company Mid Devon Therapies is run from the Carriage House by Alan Taylor.

Dipford Farm. Clockwise from top left: *Fred Webber on horse; Dorrie Webber with black pigs; Kath Webber with pet deer; Dorrie and Kath on 'Whippet', Fred's favourite horse, 1921; Kath, Dorrie and May on the granary steps, 1932); Fred haymaking at Shillingford.* Sally Luxton

DIPFORD FARM

SMILLINGFORD

**Three miles from Bampton, Four and a half
from Wiveliscombe and Eight from Tiverton**

Most important unreserved Sale of 50 cho e Devon Beasts and 2 excellent Sheep
and Lambs, a Hay Loader

KNOWLMAN & SONS

have been favoured with instructions from F. G. Webber, Esq.,
who is retiring, to SELL BY AUCTION, on THE PREMISES,

On FRIDAY, 21st MARCH, 1947

commencing with the Sheep at **1** o'clock,
the undermentioned very valuable

LIVE STOCK

comprising :

BEASTS

9 Devon Cows in calf, two of which are expected to have calves by their side by
day of sale, and the remainder forward in calf.

14 choice Devon Steers, 2 years old.

16 nice Devon Heifers, 2 years old.

6 promising Steer and Heifer yearlings

SHEEP

70 very healthy Double and Single Couples (4 and 6 teeth Ewes)

90 good Ewe and Wether Hogs.

Full mouth Ram

The Ewes are mostly cross-bred (Devon and Exmoor Horn), Lambs and Hogs by a Hampshire Down Ram

Also **HAY LOADER**

Dipford is one of the most healthy Farms in the district.   The Auctioneers can
thoroughly recommend this stock to intending purchasers.

THE GRASS OF FARM WILL BE SOLD IN APRIL

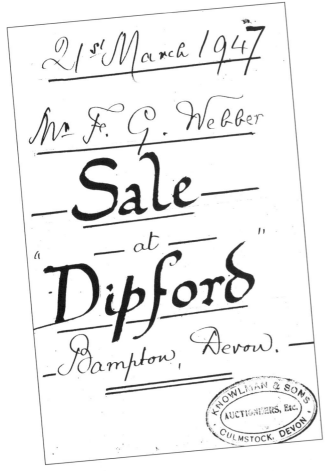

Above: *front page of document of sale for Dipford, 1947.* Top right l-r: *Dorrie May, Fred and Kathy, 1923.* Right: *Fred Webber with a powerful workhorse, 1918.*

Fred and May came to Dipford in 1911 and stayed until retiring in about 1950. A serious outbreak of foot-and-mouth disease wiped out their stock in the 1940s and Fred lost heart in his farming. When you breed and rear cattle they become a part of your life, and to see that dreaded disease wipe them out is too much for some farmers to bear.

Farming will never be the concerted efforts of manual team work seen in Fred Webber's day and before that time. When grass fields were scythed, the grass was turned by pitch fork and wooden-pronged rakes helped rew it up, to be collected loose, by horse and cart. Hay ricks were made in a corner of the field and roofed against the weather. To use the hay, one opened a part of the rick and, standing on the top of the hay, pushed a hay knife, with its triangular blade and wooden handle, downwards into the rick, keeping one's feet well apart! One then lifted out the cut chunk of hay, re-covered the rick and that was it! Fine

for one or two animals, but hard work on a big rick, feeding a large number of stock.

Sally Luxton has two of Fred's diaries. Mostly they record the everyday farm tasks of his workers but now and again May adds a bit. Such as 'Fred got thrown from a horse , and was unconcious for a few days, requiring daily visits from the doctor and the services of a night nurse as he was ranting and restless.'

Farm machinery was often belt driven and seldom had protective guards. In 1942, Fred got caught in a belt-driven machine. It stripped him bare, apart from his collar and the bands at the knee of his breeches! Although this laid him low again, Fred survived!

Horses featured in many farming stories of yesteryear, as in the next tale.

Whilst out hunting on the cliffs at Glenthorn, bewteen Porlock and Lynmouth, Fred Webber was with several other riders. One of note was Lady Munnings (collectors of sporting paintings will recall one of the famous artists of earlier this century was Sir Alfred Munnings).

In the course of the chase, Lady Munnings was thrown from her horse which fell over the cliffs which are steep and covered with vegetation and some trees. Fred was the person who opted to rescue the horse. Somehow he got the frightened animal off the cliffs where a delighted Sir Alfred offered Fred a choice as a reward. Either he could have the next painting that he finished or a case of whisky. Yes, Fred chose the latter!

Bampton was one of many markets in the area. Some sold fatstock and little in the way of store animals, while others sold less fatstock.

Retired farmer, Bertie Evans, remembers markets at Brushford, East Anstey Brompton Regis, Exford and Tiverton, as well as at Bampton. The last monthly Bampton market was in the late 1960s, after which the Christmas Fatstock Cup was passed to the Bampton Young Farmers Club for annual competition. Bampton market was originally run by Knowlman Brothers who, in the 1950s, became Dobbs and Knowlman, then Dobbs, Stag and Knowlman. In the 1980s it reverted to Stags.

Competition was always keen among local farmers to see who would 'top' the prices for that day in either sheep or cattle, fat or stores. Much the same as it is today. Markets are bigger now as farmers have fewer to choose from. Weekly markets are held at Taunton, Exeter and South Molton. Some open twice a week. Apart from general livestock markets, these three, along with Cutcombe on Exmoor, hold annual sheep auctions where several thousand are sold in one day. Raleighs Cross on the Brendon Hills used to be another big sheep auction. A twice-yearly sheep and cattle fair is recorded at Winsford in 1860.

A sheep market at Bampton in July 1953. Photo Rosemary Woodward

TIVERTON STAGHOUNDS

For many farmers the hunt was the only way some country folk could spend a few hours off work. Bosses and employees both enjoyed a day's hunting and many packs of hounds still are kennelled on or around Exmoor, and the Tiverton Staghounds were once kennelled at Duvale, Bampton.

The Tiverton Staghounds were started in 1896 by Sir John Amory who put his son, Ian, in charge as Master and Huntsman. For fourteen years Ian hunted the hounds, until 1910, when John Amory gave them up and his brother, Captain Harry Amory, who lived at Brushford, near Dulverton, took the hunt over. At the outbreak of war, in 1914, many hounds had to be put down and the hunt kept going with a smaller pack under the care of Charlie Slater from 1915. He lived at Hatch, South Molton.

In 1919 the Hunt moved to Bampton with the Yandle Family. Jack was the brains behind the scenes and Master of the Hunt, while his younger two brothers, Percy and Bert, hunted the pack on alternate days.

Percy, a bachelor, stayed and farmed at Duvale, while the fourth brother lived at Riphay, Exebridge. Bert Yandle married Nina and farmed at Fitzhead, and at Boobier here at Bampton. In about 1948 Bert built a house at Woodrow. Aubrey Besley who used to work with the Yandles as a lad said:

Woodrow is one of the most beautiful spots you can imagine. Tucked high up behind the Exeter Inn it is so warm being snuggled under the hill and facing south-west. But the best part in those days was to watch the lovely steam trains going up and down the line. You could hear them whistle at Cove and watch them coming up the line towards Bampton. It was such a wonderful sight with the steam pouring out of the funnel, way down below us in the meadow.
It was a privilege to know the Yandles, as they were a real country family who worked hard, and adamantly believed in hunting being the only way to ensure the survival of the red deer.

Percy kept the hounds at Duvale until once more war broke out and many hounds had to be put down. Again a skeleton pack kept going and the hunt moved to another location. Bert and Nina had one son, Jim, who was a familiar figure seen cycling the Exe Valley. Their hunting 'country'

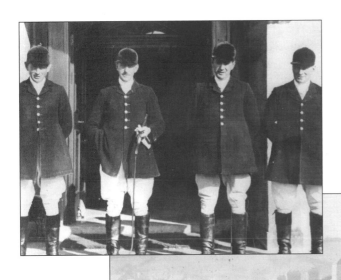

Left: Jack Ernest and Percy Yandle. Photo Richard Lethbridge.

Below: *Huntsmen bringing ponies into Bampton, probably for the Fair. Note the hurdles at the road-side.* Mrs Currie

Bottom: *Aubrey Besley leads the Tiverton Staghounds from a meet at the Jubilee Inn, 1960s.* Photo Richard Lethbridge

had more roads than the Devon and Somerset Staghounds, covering Bampton area in the north and Chulmleigh in the south. Rackenford Moor was boggy and rough, but a favourite spot for the red deer. Nowadays the North Devon Link Road runs across it, but it is possible still to see the deer in fields adjacent to the new road.

The Yandle family continue to farm at Riphay today. Aubrey Besley took over the Tiverton Staghounds acting as Master and Huntsman for eleven years. He was a popular person during this time being able to communicate easily with people of all ages. Both Aubrey and his wife Mary continue to take a keen interest in the hunt.

Diana Thomas whose husband farms Sparkhayne at Bampton said the family residence there goes back to 1892. She wrote for this book:

On the 2 August 1892, Caroline Thomas with her son, John Thomas, came from Snydles Farm, Umberleigh, to Sparkhayne, Bampton. John later married Nellie Bowden from Gumbland Farm, Bampton, and they had the following children: Edith 1895, William 1898, Francis 1900, Gilbert 1903, Doris 1904, Lionel 1908 Vera 1912, and Arthur 1914.

John Thomas died in 1916, aged 48 years and so Nellie continued to farm at Sparkhayne and bring up her eight children. Nellie died in 1933, aged 59 years, and the farm was eventually taken over by Gilbert, who married Ethel Evered on 1 January 1942. They had a son and daughter. When Gilbert died in1975 Christopher took over the farm where he lives with his wife Diana.

The farm comprises 222 acres and runs 100 cattle, 500 sheep, 40 acres of cereals and fifteen acres of swedes for human consumption. During Christopher's lifetime on the farm, farming has changed from horses, wagons, and lots of manual workers who toiled long hours all the year round, to contractors who bring round balers, lifting equipment, combines, swede harvesters, etc. Work that once took weeks is now done in hours.

Thomas family wedding c.1925. Men l-r: *Gilbert, Arthur, Francis-William, and Lionel.* Women l-r: *Doris, Edith, Caroline and Vera.* Photo Diana Thomas

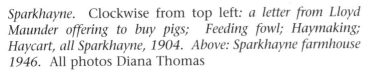

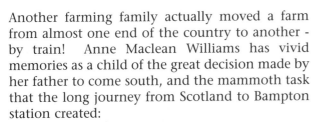

Sparkhayne. Clockwise from top left: *a letter from Lloyd Maunder offering to buy pigs; Feeding fowl; Haymaking; Haycart, all Sparkhayne, 1904. Above: Sparkhayne farmhouse 1946.* All photos Diana Thomas

Another farming family actually moved a farm from almost one end of the country to another - by train! Anne Maclean Williams has vivid memories as a child of the great decision made by her father to come south, and the mammoth task that the long journey from Scotland to Bampton station created:

On 25 September, 1955 I undertook the most exciting journey of my young life at that time. My father; Alec McLean Bullen, had sold his dairy farm in Ayrshire, Scotland, and bought Wonham Barton, Bampton. He hired a whole train from British Railways for £400 to move all the live-stock, machinery - and his children! - my brother, Ted (19), in charge of the train, my sister, Dorothy (17), and me (7). We had a standard passenger carriage and slept on the long seats.

We milked our herd of Ayrshire cows in Scotland before walking them to Glengarnock station to be loaded on to the railcars. We also had the collies, cats and hens. My parents had gone on ahead to Devon in the car.

It was fascinating watching the countryside roll by and I recall sticking my head out of the window at Carlisle at 6 o'clock on a dark, misty

morning and asking why our train had stopped. The railwayman said 'the train is too heavy, you'll need a second engine to pull it'. We finally arrived at Bampton station on 25 September 1955 in the early afternoon. I remember thinking there were a lot of people watching us arrive.

Diana Thorns of Sparkhayne recalls seeing all the cattle trucks in the railway sidings. We, unloaded, the cows and walked them up the hill to High Cross, past Benshayes where Leonard White farmed (his son Geoff and his family still live there today), and past Westbrook where the late Mr and Mrs Pearson farmed with their daughters, Sylvia and Esme (who now live in Bampton), and so to Wonham Barton. The cows were milked and turned out in the field.

The Devon and Somerset News came and took a photograph; the arrival, of this Scottish family end all their cows seemed to be quite an event. People still mention my father's train today. For me it was an epic journey.

Wonham Barton has since been passed to me. I married Clifford Henry Williams of Bittiscombe Hill, Raddington on 8 April 1989, at a service in Bampton church. Michael Rendell played the organ for us and Gerry Berrow played the bagpipes as we left St Michael and All Angels, thus preserving our Scottish family tradition as my sister, Dorothy, had bagpipes played in April, 1966 when she married Arthur George Mogford of Stockham Farm, Dulverton. My brother returned to Scotland and farms with his family in Aberdeenshire.

We subsequently discovered, by chance, that Clifford's grandfather, Bill Williams, farmed and lived at Wonham Barton from 1912 to 1916, and some of my husband's aunts can remember the old water wheel working to grind the corn. For us, therefore, it is a happy coincidence that there is a Williams once again at Wonham Barton after eighty years.

Farming has undergone many changes in the past forty years since I came from Scotland, but Wonham Barton is still a thriving agricultural business in Bampton Parish.

Alan Rowland is a most familiar face around Bampton. He lives at Wick Farm not far from Diana and Christopher Thomas. Samuel Rowland, Alan's grandfather came to Bampton originally as a police sergeant. He liked the look of Bampton so much that he decided to rent Wick Farm in 1919. From then he built Exeview and Highfield, in High Street, and moved into Exeview. Sam and Laura had a son, Hedley, Alan's father.

Grandad Rowland on the beat in Paignton, 1931. Photo A. Rowland.

Hedley had married May and moved into Wick Farm in 1926. The farm was only small but mixed farming was achieved. Hedley and a friend Bill Sully began an egg, poultry and rabbit collection at Wick. At one stage rabbits were plentiful enough to provide enough income to pay the rent.

Alan like many other local lads joined Bampton Young Farmers when he was aged about sixteen. It has always been a competitive club, covering all aspects of farming: hedging, ditching, stockmanship, tractor miantainence, etc. Alan soon found himself in the club team for inter-club and national competitions. There were catergories of county competitions at that time: quizes, public speaking and drama. Alan represented the club in all three. Pam and Shirley Greenslade, Evelyn Gibbons, Rob Venner, Percy Hill and Alan made up the winning quiz team.

Public speaking teams included Doreen Rawle, Rob Venner, and John Perkins. Something to do on dark winter evenings produced the fun of practising for drama competitions. Today those starlets are a trifle bashful, but admit it all was great fun.

Percy Hill and Alan decided that they would like to compete at the Royal Show in the Senior National Tool and Machinery competition. The Royal Show at that time toured the country, each year and, in 1952, it was to be in Newton Abbot.

The Royal Agricultural Society certificate awarded to Alan Rowland and Percy Hill, 1953.

Below: *Bampton Young Farmers Club Show, c.1952. L-r: Evelyn Gibbons; Kathleen Holloway; Frank Hollway; John Wensley; John Palfrey. Onlookers include Bert Yandel, John Bucknell's mother, Betty Crockford, Charlie and Wilf Kelland, Percy Hill, Sam Rowland, Mr Chamberlain, John Penwarden and Ern Gillard.*

Left: *Bampton Young Farmers Club Show 1953, held in the Market Field. L-r: John Gooding; Evelyn Gibbons; Mr Sellick; Alan Rowland; Mr W, Frankpitt, Betty Palfrey. All photos Alan Rowland*

These two Scrooges decided if they competed they would get in free!

The qualifying round was at Shepton Mallett, where the two Bampton lads won the South West area, qualifying for the final at Newton Abbot. A third place in the final was a good result for Bampton.

Farming is full of ups and downs but Alan has enjoyed the life and the challenges. Now his son Colin has joined him and hopes to keep the business going.

There is another farmer who, like Alan Rowland, is a well known face in Bampton on a Friday when he does his shopping. Tom Phillips, who farms Surridge Farm, had the misfortune to lose his wife Ethel a few years ago. Prior to that sad

Photographs from June Palfrey (née Phillips) who farms at Ashtown. Clockwise from top left: Tom and Ethel Phillips on the wedding day, May 1939. Tom and Ethel's family at Foxhanger. John Palfrey senior on the tractor at Ashtown. Stooking corn at Ashtown l-r: David Palfrey; John Palfrey (on trailer); Frank Parkman.

time people seldom saw Tom away from his farm He milks a herd of cows twice a day just as he has for sixty-five years, and keeps a flock of sheep. Nothing too unusual in that, I hear you say? Maybe not, farmers all work hard and at present have all the odds stacked against making a successful income.

But Tom Phillips *is* different in that he is 84 years old and, regularly as clockwork, starts milking at 2am every day! He jokes when asked why 2am - 'Call it mad cow disease!'

For 43 years Tom has lived at Surridge and kept up to 200 cows on two farms. He milks about 70 while the others, on the second farm, are milked by his son, Monty.

He recalls a really bad week, soon after marrying Ethel, and buying his own farm:

It was one of those times when at first you accept one problem as part of farming, two is a bit rough, when after that it gets grim! It began with a bought-in cow that went 'scanter'. That meant it

Bill Payne ploughing at Whitehall, Morebath, 1932.

had Johnnes Disease, with culling the only option. That cow went on a Monday morning. The same day, on fetching the cows from the field for milking, I found one dead in the river. On Tuesday I lost two sheep and a bullock. On Saturday, still in the same week, I went to get the horse and saw it 'wasn't right', so I called the vet. When he arrived I opened the stable door and the horse dropped dead beside me! He was a lovely horse too. Sunday morning I found two pigs dead from something I put in their feed. So I said, that if I ever had another week like that one I would pack up and go away!

Fortunately Tom stayed farming and he and Ethel had seven children. Monty and June both farm close to Surridge. Ray, Colin, Dave and Shirley he sees quite often, while Brenda set up home in New Zealand.

Tom says he might take time off when he gets to 100 years, but would get bored sitting by a window waiting to die!

Tom Phillips. BS

It was the sale of sheep that originally brought Bampton Fair to prominence. Newton Square 1890. RK

People and animals mingle in the crowded streets at Bampton Fair, around 1920. RK

Chapter 8 - Bampton Fair

Ask any local how they remember the old Bampton Fair Day and a variety of answers will pour forth, including the main one of RAIN, RAIN, AND MORE RAIN! Other memories will be of timid ponies, cattle, sheep, crowds, noise, gypsies telling your future and drunks fighting in the pubs and inns. All these memories usually come before the thoughts of bargains and happy gatherings, as friends and relatives visited for the day. For the women it was a busy week baking large apple tarts and skinning saucepans of potatoes, usually eaten with home-boiled ham and homemade chutney.

The day does have a stigma of gloomy weather, yet look at all the photographs going back generations and ask, 'where is all that rain?'

Even so, mud has been deep enough to lose one's footwear in the old market field, where Market Close is now built, but what about the time of the unmade roads? Imagine them wet, and rough, together with all the animal excrement, as hundreds, even thousands of animals were sold on the streets among all the crowds!

Look at the pictures! Sheep sales in Newton Square, cattle loose in Brook Street and, later, as the sheep trade died, horses and ponies driven on foot through the streets. Poor little ponies straight from the peace of Exmoor suddenly surrounded by buildings, people and noise. No wonder properties were boarded-up (for the princely sum of l/6d).

Arnold Seward remembers:

Exmoor ponies were driven in on foot from Simonsbath, Anstey Common, Molland Moor and Winsford Hill, several hundred came to be sold for only half a crown, or maybe double that, five shillings. There were several places selling animals at the same time. Ponies were sold in Briton Street and in the paddock behind the Tiverton Hotel. Bullocks were sold in Frog Street and Castle street. Sheep were sold in West Street and in the Market Field, where Market Close stands today, and of course they had been sold outside the bakery in Newton Square. Many private houses sold refreshments as well as the shops.

Lots of noise from colourful cheap-jack stalls com-bined with stallholders shouting relentlessly to try and attract customers for their special offers of the day. Arnold recalls.

At first for the older part of the Fair Day history it was a most serious event. It was the chance to sell stock from your farm and pay up all accounts while planning the next year's work. Huge crowds flocked into the town. For many farm folk it was their only day out in a year. Many came on foot, as the men walked their animals several miles to be sold here. The family would later have come by pony and trap (though one story that women were not supposed to come to the Fair until late in the 1800s, remains questionable). There were early amusement stalls in the form of bare-fist boxing and wrestling, although the Fun Fair did not become part of the day until much later. Jones roundabouts were in the entrance to the Market field in about1920. At first they were brought by horse-drawn vehicles, then traction engines and later motors.

Another link with Fair people and Bampton was in September, when on a Sunday the Show (Fair) people came through Bampton travelling from Barnstaple Fair to Bridgewater Fair. All were horse-drawn vehicles. The caravans were too wide to go down Back Street, so they had to go round Fore Street. Castle Hill was short but very steep and slippery so locals used to go out and help the horses up the hill. It took all day. Later then they all returned to Bampton for our Fair Day.

It was a meeting of old friends each year as Fair families shopped with us year after year and we in return visited their stalls or amusements.

It would seem there were markets or fairs long before the Domesday Book appeared. Twenty-three sheep and fifty goats are listed in Bampton at that time. By the end of the 1300s Bampton was second only to Barnstaple in importance in the Devon cloth-making industry. By the late 1700s or early 1800s the October Fair was the largest in the West Country and 14 000 sheep were sold! One can only wonder how such a vast number were catered for, it really is an unimaginable amount of animals to be in Bampton on just one day!

Bampton Fair

Almost a century separates these two scenes of the Fair in Briton Street, the top picture taken in 1890 and the lower picture in 1980. RK

Bampton Fair

Two other contrasting views, the top picture shows the pony sale in progress at the Tiverton Hotel c.1900, the lower picture is the same sale ring 60 years later. RK

In the ensuing 100 years this number dramatically dropped to around 200 as the wool and cloth industry waned. As has been mentioned earlier, Bampton actually had its own breed of sheep, the Bampton Nott. In fact Bampton was famed for this large type sheep; sadly there seems to be no photographs of the breed and it is supposed to have been interbred with Leicestershires to form the Devon Longwool. They gave a fleece of about 12lbs.

At around this time the pony trade began to join the cattle and sheep earnest, the ponies being the sturdy Exmoor breed. Dulverton Fair and one in Tiverton either died out or grew smaller in size leaving Bampton the busiest horse and pony fair around. Trade in ponies and horses grew and somewhere around 2000 animals filled the streets.

The Knight family of Simonsbath brought the first ponies on foot, a distance of at least twenty miles. When the railway became part of Bampton life in 1884 the wool trade was weakening and Exmoor ponies, which had become part of the fair trade about 1856, travelled by train instead of the long treks on the hoof. After sale they were sent to work in the Welsh mines and travelled by train from Bampton Station. During the weeks preceeding the Fair, empty animal trucks were accumulated at Bampton's sidings in readiness for that purpose. As time passed by animal pens were built, first to be used in Newton Square for any animal, and later in an orchard to the right of the

Seahorse Inn, then called the Tiverton Hotel. Here pony sales continued from the early 1940s until their demise in 1985.

Bargain bedding and china could, and still can be, bought from stalls piled high with tempting bankrupt and end-of-range, stock. The best bargains were reckoned to be offered for stalwart folk still around at 11pm. Many a resident waited for Fair Day to replenish their cupboards.

Masses of stalls crowded Brook Street and sometimes their awnings used almost to meet overhead in the narrowest parts, where the huge crowds often came to a standstill, packed like sardines. Definitely not an experience for the faint hearted.

You could buy just about anything at the Fair, from christmas cards to the latest household gadget, or from a goat to a carthorse in bygone days.

Local businesses were open, hoping most farmers would pay their accounts before having a beer in one of the many pubs, each vying for trade. Bampton had thirteen pubs at one time. Even today the pubs and hotels strip their bars so that if the day is wet with rain and mud, or just spilt ale, it will be easily cleaned up. The large quantities of scrumpy cider consumed at Bampton Fair, was the likely cause for many a red face, and an awful lot of tall stories.

Tolls charged for Bampton Fair Day in 1968 were: Ponies 4d per head, bullocks 6d per head, sheep 2/6d per score. All stalls and commercial

Though much damaged, this rare photograph give a sense of the turmoil that existed in the days when Bampton Fair attracted massive crowds of both people and animals. Private houses as well as the usual traders did great business, the building on the left advertises 'Hot Dinner'. RK

Bampton Fair

Briton Street, c. 1920, Note the Sentinel lorry on the right, possibly one of Scotts'. Photo Mrs Currie

Another view of Briton Street, taken at around the same time. RK

Below: *The display of wonderful head-gear date this picture to around 1910. In the background stalls can be seen on the left hand side of the street, while the gilded frame on the left is possibly part of a fun fair booth. The ladders, presumably, were for sale.* RK

Bampton Fair

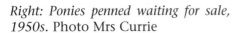

Fair Day c.1920. Just imagine the noise, the smell and the bustle of the crowd. RK

Right: Ponies penned waiting for sale, 1950s. Photo Mrs Currie

Below: *Following their sale at the Tiverton Hotel, ponies are driven through the streets on the way to Bampton railway station where cattle trucks waited to take them away. Many were used as pit ponies in the South Wales coalmines.* RK

This interesting photograph, taken in Luke Street in the 1920s, shows the preparations made to protect houses from the crush of cattle and horses as they were driven through the streets.

displays 2 shillings per foot of road frontage, 7 shillings for every mobile salesman and 7/6d for every caravan parked in connection with the Fair (information supplied by Mrs Phyll Marley the present Toll Collector).

When Mr Baxter was Lord of the Manor, to whom all Tolls were due, he leased the Bampton Fair Tolls to the Town Council on the understanding that they would be distributed between local organisations.

Wonderful characters were regularly seen among the menfolk who leant on the animal pens, yarning about the previous twelve months misfortunes and rigours of farming. These great people worked hard on their farms without any of the mod cons of today. There were few machines, horses were trusted to help work the land in a slow and laborious way, but with a great pride in achievement. This is something that will never be repeated and deserves special mention in any history book. Come wind, storm, snow or drought, these wonderful animals toiled with their master. And at the end of an exhausting day,

horses had to be bedded down before the farmer could call it a day.

Let us look closely at those wonderful little Exmoor ponies. They are recognised by their rich brown colour, not a white hair to be seen in the purest ponies. They all have a light-coloured (mealy) muzzle and underparts. The brand of their owner is clearly seen on their summer coat, such as an anchor with a number beneath it, as on some of the Winsford Hill ponies.

Though they are robust enough for light adults, they are not ideal for children, as they can be strong-willed, and perhaps not smart enough for the modern child to be seen riding. Yet their stamina proved to be almost limitless during their working life of long ago.

On Exmoor today there are wild herds, all owned by someone, or the Exmoor National Park. Fortunately the Exmoor differ from the Dartmoor pony by being shy of humans, thus limiting the numbers killed on the moorland roads. Others are dotted around the country, kept by admirers

Bampton Fair

Originally the Fair was essentially a place to buy and sell, and the entertainment side of the day came later. Here the employees of George Davey & Sons exhibit their business wares in Silver Street, c.1900. RK

Stallholders attract the crowds in Brook Street in the 1960s. Photo Dorothy Ellicott.

The Exmoor pony in its native habitat. Author

At sales they used to fetch a few shillings and now in their decline they can be bought for a few pounds. Strange how these wonderful ponies are so closely associated with the Fair when they were not sold here until about 1856

The Charter for Bampton Fair was confirmed by Henry III to the first vicar of Bampton, Osmund, in 1258, almost seven-and-a-half centuries ago. Today's Fair Day is quite different from that of days gone by. Some people are dismissive of the modern Fair Day, but most Bamptonians would not want to see this tradition fade out completely and various ideas are being tried to stimulate greater interest. The main suggestion to change the date in lieu of better weather cannot work as the Charter holds the Fair to the last Thursday in October.

y[Gone today are the pony sales, the cattle and sheep sales, but the street market still functions, although with a great reduction in the type and number of stalls. Not only were there stalls in Brook Street, in recent years they filled all parts of Fore Street, Newton Square, and all Luke Street, including both sides of the roads all round the island. Station Road, the top end of Barnhay linking into West Street, had stalls too! Then came the recession and the new health and hygiene regulations, and stalls vanished in large numbers.

of the breed. Even in the show ring, unless it is competing against its own breed, the precious Exmoor pony is seldom given a second glance, as the Welsh types are more eye-catching and extravagant in their action, preferred by many judges.

Yet it still is, and probably always will be known as Bampton Pony Fair and it is sure to be WET!

Bampton pony sale ring at the back of the Tiverton Hotel, 1981. RK

Bampton Tennis Club 1930s.

Bampton Football Club, 1920, at the Cup Final played on the Athletic Ground, Tiverton. **Standing l-r:** *Tom Lazarus, Dr Fisher, Clarke, Sewell, Bill Hagley, Harry Clode, Jimmy Gage, Frank Staddon.* **Kneeling:** *Jack Herniman; Harry Hancock; Mont Napper; Bob Burnett; Frank Dyer (Huntsham); H, Hooper (Huntsham).* **Front row:** *Harry Clode jnr; Tommy Denscombe; Bert Gregory; Fred Miles; Jim Palmer (Huntsham); Frank Yeo.* RK

Chapter 9 - Sport and Recreation

Bampton never has been anything other than, busy, self sufficient, pleasant and friendly to live, while offering many opportunities in leisure activities for all ages. Of course in every place someone will be heard to moan about lack of facilities, but really over the years Bampton has offered a good selection, without the need to travel out of the town.

Today the trend is to try and educate people to keep fit and active, and no better opportunities have been offered than in sport over the years. Some of the earlier clubs have gone, but different ones have been formed to replace them.

FOOTBALL

Established Bampton families have been represented for many years in Bampton Association Football Club. The club has thrived and gained many successes in its history. The names of Reg Kingdon and his two brothers, Raymond and

Craig Woodman, talented young footballer.

Bernard keep popping up in the records as do many others. At the time of writing the first team has gained promotion so the competitive spirit flourishes and a youth team is set to look for league fixtures next season. These youngsters will be the backbone of the senior club in the next century. As always there are some keen fathers to thank for helping to run the club.

One young man who is currently making a name for himself in the game of football is Craig Woodman. Following the love for the game through his father, Chris, who played for Bampton, Craig has signed to play for Bristol City. The initial trial period saw many miles clocked up as his parents drove up and back from Bristol. It was all worth it as they are delighted to see their son succeed in the sport. At present Craig is at Lilleshall, England School of Excellence for Sport.

The encouragement of adults brings on the younger talent, and this has happened in Bampton for years. Through the generous sponsorship of local businesses kit is bought and proudly worn, by a First and Reserve Team.

Football today is played beneath the Motte mound. It used to be played in the field beside Shillingford Road Garage.

CRICKET, TENNIS AND BILLIARDS

Bampton used to have a strong cricket club, a tennis club, and billiards club. Bert Hookins was a great billiard player and the game was played in what is now St Michael's Hall and above the library in the Manor Room in the Constitutional Club, and in the room behind the White Horse Hotel. Bert was an accomplished player who regularly captained the Devon county team.

RUNNING

Over the last few years electrician Paul Burnett has organised a 10-km run for those feeling more athletic. It usually starts and finishes at the recreation field and proceeds are given to Bampton youth organisations. This year 118 runners took part and for the first time, Anne Sanders, present chairman of the Town Council, organised a Fun Run on the same night.

Sport and Recreation

Bampton Junior Football Team 1912-13. RK

Bampton Football Team at Court Green, 1921. L-r: Charlie Hutter; Ern Salisbury; Bert Cleeve; Horace Nott; Harry Clode; Mont Napper; Tommy Denscombe; Harry Dyer; Bert Gregory; Fred Toze; Jack Cockram. RK

Bampton National School (Brook Street) Football Team 1921-22. Standing l-r: Lionel Thomas, Ern Serenger; Lionel Hancock; Reg Toze; Jack Heal; Reg Milton; Bill Collard; C. Gage; H. Cottrell; Len Bowden; E. Gage. Headmaster Mr Shenton and the Revd Cox.

Sport and Recreation

Bampton AFC 1925-26 - the Walrond Cup-winning team, played at the Athletic Ground, Tiverton, against Cullompton, winning 1–0. Standing l-r: F. Tooze (standing in for Vic Tuckfield); George Hutter; Bill Taylor; Arthur Lawrence; Frank Gibbings and Percy Hancock. Sitting l-r: Leonard Kingdom; Don Atkins; Bob Burnett; Len Burnett (Capt.); Mont Napper; Don Gould; Mr Kingdom.

Bampton AFC around 1948. Standing l-r: G. Hutter; B. Hodge; A. Collard; R.J. Kingdon; W. Turnbull; E. Kerslake; S. Coles; F. Gibbings; E. Alderman. Sitting l-r: A. Rooks; J. Matthews; B. Kingdon; F. Bishop; A. Gibbings; A. Denscombe; George Chamberlain. RK

Below: Bampton AFC First XI, 1948-49. Standing l-r: Donald Gould (Hon. Sec.); Bernard Kingdon; Alan Collard; Bill Turnbull; Reg Kingdon; Ern Kerslake; Cyril Chidgey; Len Gratton. Kneeling: Derick Dunn; Johnny Matthews; Bernard Hodge; Arthur Gibbings; Jack Parkhouse. RK

Bampton Rifle Club, around 1950. Standing: *Michael Rendell; Gerry Vile; Les Coles; Dudley Weatherley.* Sitting: *unknown; Frank Manley; Evan Collacott; Humphrey Weston; Reg Yendell.* Photo Joy Coles.

PIGEON RACING

For many years Bampton skies have been full of racing pigeons, exercising before circling over their lofts. The Exmoor Border Flying Club was founded by Arnold Seward and other fanciers, with some extremely keen members whose pigeons flew home in races from France and Spain as well as shorter British routes. It is an incredible sight to see huge pigeon transporters release thousands of birds together. There still are local people flying pigeons, now under a different club name.

RIDING AND HUNTING

Hunting has been a popular sport for centuries with several packs of hounds in the Bampton area. Ponies and horses are a common sight in the fields surrounding Bampton. Some people only ride around the lanes, while a few enjoy the show ring. The author has a wonderful elderly mare, Tawstock Caroline, who gave her a big thrill by becoming champion at Devon County Show, as a brood mare with a filly foal at foot.

One young man who has made his career with horses is Luke Harvey, whose family home was

'Grandad' Seward, as Arnold was known for the last thirty years, with two of his award-winning racing pigeons. BS

Luttrell Farm, Bampton. Luke is a presenter on the Television Racing Channel and is also seen on Sky Television's Winning Post summer evening racing programme. He is still a competent National Hunt Jockey, too! Possibly his greatest

Luke Harvey at Hereford Races riding Final Sound, owned by Brian Seward and John Davis

race win was the Welsh Grand National on Cool Ground for Toby Balding.

Luke has ridden all kinds of ponies all his life as his parents bought and sold them. One pony Luke rode for some time was not exactly placid. In fact Sundance gave young Luke some hairy experiences. Once out hunting as a small lad two Bamptonians met him on a path in the middle of a wood, with his pony bridle in his hand. Luke asked them if they had seen the pony as it had dumped him and carried on! Another time the same two people were riding across a field. 'Mind the sack on the ground,' one called to the other as they approached the gateway. On arriving at the gateway, the sack was little Luke, knocked out cold, not a pony in sight!

BAMPTON HORSE SHOW

For many years Bampton Gymkhana was a big event, organised by Roland Scott. For a few days each year the familiar Scotts lorries could be seen hauling brightly-coloured show jumps instead of stone. The gymkhana took place in Mr Weston's field behind Shillingford Road Garage, drawing crowds of 2000 people and competitors in show-jumping of international standard. From here, a youthful Derek Ricketts, who having qualified at Bampton for the Leading Young Rider competition, went on to win the National Final at the Horse of the Year Show in 1967. George Hobbs was another famous name. Bampton Gymkhana in the 1960s also held a qualifying round for the Foxhunter Competition.

When Mr. Scott retired the event became Bampton Horse Show, run at Wick Farm by Sheila and Alan Rowland for 24 years. They also kennelled the pack of Holcombe Rogus Beagles. The hounds are now kennelled elsewhere.

SHEEPDOG TRIALS

Every shepherd thinks he has the best sheepdog in the world. Well, most of them do! To try and prove it some compete in Sheepdog Trials, and there is an annual trial in Bampton, run by Mrs Anne Williams. It was held near the Wishing Well house (formerly a café) on the Taunton Road. Bampton Sheepdog Trials has an avid supporter in Bertie Evans of Shillingford. Bertie has trained over a hundred dogs during his life and became one of the best known competitors in the area, frequently being asked to give demonstrations with his dogs.

Sport and Recreation

Bertie Evans with his sheepdog Kim, Champions at the Somerset and Avon Sheepdog Trials, 1977.

Below: *Bampton Secondary Modern School Football Team 1953-54. Standing l-r: Gerald Hancock; Ted Hutters; Ron Stoneman; Brian Buckingham; Tony Saunders; Clifford Stamp. Sitting l-r: Michael Snell; Raymond Harper; Derick Wensley; Len Sampson; Ken Jones; Michael Gardner. RK*

Sport and Recreation

Joyce Taylor (later Joyce Kingdon), Bampton Football Queen, 1948. RK

Below: *Bampton openers, Len Venn and Reg Kingdon, go out to bat at Bridgetown, 1959. Other Bampton players in the photo are: Cliff and George Coles, Cliff Fowler, Gordon Cockram, Tony Toze, John Reed.* RK

OTHER CLUBS AND INTERESTS

Other leisure interests in Bampton come in good variety. A thriving Over 60's Club, founded by Arnold Seward, has a good membership and they are given ample opportunities to travel on excursions during the summer.

The Horticultural Club was running in 1869 and the more recent members ran two flower shows each year and had their sales room on Castle Hill. That club folded to be replaced by the Plant and Garden Society.

There is a Bampton Society whose preliminary letter invited people to join in 1989. It has monthly meetings when speakers cover many topics linked with Bampton and our area. Even on how I set about collating this book!

One of the most enduring organisations in Bampton and rural areas throughout the country is the WI. Bampton's Women's Institute, whose scrapbook I have used for this book, is a cornerstone of community life. Bampton Monday Club provide a pleasant night out each month, while Bampton pre-School and Toddler Groups give an opportunity for young mothers to get together with their children.

Bampton also offers American Line Dancing and Short Mat Bowling activities, while Bampton Rifle Club has a long history of excellent shots, with members shooting for Devon

The Mother's Union is long established, while Bampton Players (drama group) have increased productions through a flourishing membership in recent years.

For those who want to get out of Bampton without driving, the Over 60's Club, Dorothy Hemming, and Seward's Spar Stores, all arrange outings to theatres and places of interest.

The hope of many people in Bampton is that the building of a Community Centre will be a real possiblity in the future. A purpose-built premises with a swimming pool and maybe an all-weather sports pitch would draw families from a wide area and, who knows what talent for the future might be uncovered. Scotts Quarries site is for sale but the cost of purchasing the site and then building and equipping a centre would be prohibitive in so small a community without an injection of some sort of public funding. It really is one project my husband and I would love to see happen.

Sport and Recreation

Bampton AFC First XI 1964-65. Standing l-r: Dennis Blackwell; Alan Taylor; Merv Williams; Jack Davis; Keith Cleeve; Merv Taylor; Des Prescott. Kneeling l-r: Brian Ridgeway; Ray Stoneman; John Gullidge; Ken Hutching; Danny Penney. RK

Bampton AFC 1972-73. Standing l-r: Derek Warren; Philip Ven; Chris Hollick; Cliff Coles; Eric Blackwell; Mike Stubbington; Gordie Mounce; Ron Bawden. Kneeling l-r: Gerald Mounce; Ken Blackwell; Merv Taylor; Danny Penney; Vernon Kingdon. RK

Sport and Recreation

Bampton AFC First XI, 1981-82. Standing l-r: *Andy Sidebottom; Mike Stubbington; Andy Bolt; Stuart Coles; Alan Crosby; Robin Woodman.* Kneeling l-r: *John Kelland; Phil Venn; Dennis King; Peter Birch; John Bircham.* both photos RK

Bampton AFC 1985. Presentation of new kit sponsored by Rotolok. Standing l-r: *Garry Llewellyn; Brian Edworthy; Andy Sidebottom; Reg Kingdon (Hon. Treasurer); Dan MacCauley (Chairman of Rotolok); Merv Taylor (Team Manager); Robin Scott; Bill Gutteridge; Peter Birch (Captain); Julian Coles.* Kneeling l-r: *Tim Riley; Kepler Wright; Andrew Hole; Martin Stoneman; Paul Smarridge; Dean Fowler.*

Sport and Recreation

Bampton Cricket Club 1956, Tiverton Town Minor Knock-out Cup winners, beating Heathcoat Apprentices in the final. Gordon Cockram won the bowling cup and Reg Kingdon the batting cup. Standing l-r: George Coles; Tony Toze; Merv Taylor; Ray Kingdon; Gordon Cockram; Edward Gannon; Len Venn. Sitting l-r: Charlie Sowden; Bernard Kingdon; Reg Kingdon (Captain); Ray Stoneman, Cliff Fowler. RK

Bampton Cricket Club Jumble Sale 1959. L-r: Charlie Sowden; Bob Alderman; Ray Kingdon; Joyce Kingdon; Beryl Kingdon; Anne Collard; Alice Taylor; Reg Kingdon; Mary Venn; Tony Toze; Margaret Kingdon; Merv Taylor; Shirley Kingdon; Bernard Kingdon; Cathy Sowden; Eddie Gannon; Violet Parkhouse. RK

Sport and Recreation

Tiverton Hotel Darts House Cup, 1967. L-r: Danny Penney; John Williams; Brendan Taylor; Merv Williams; Jack Davis; Bill Taylor; Merv Taylor (winner); Cliff Fowler; Dick Gould (Landlord); Watney's Rep; Colin Green; Reg Kingdon (runner-up); Mick Aldridge; Paul Severn; Gilbert Gratton. RK

Runners at the start of the 10 kilometre run, 1997. The event, sponsored by Burnett Electrical Services and Spar, raised £300 for local Guides, Scouts and Brownies. BS

Sport and Recreation

Bampton Football Team 1994-95. Standing l-r: D. Penney; unknown; S. Chamberlain; Graham Seatherton; Vernon Kingdon; Andy Sidebottom; James Davey; Peter Bage. Front row l-r: Robert Hagley; Mike Soutcott; Jerry Kelland; Paul Gould; Mark Freemantle. RK

Above: Bampton Over 60s Club day outing to Looe and Polperro 1988. Mrs Westcott; Muriel Heard; Joy Coles; Norman Cleverley; Vera Gibbings and Joyce Kingdon.

Left: Tiverton and District Billiards and Snooker Leage, 1970s. Back l-r: Eric Shillabeer; Sam Pengelley. Front l-r: Charlie Ridgeway; Bert Hookins; 'Tich' Gardner. RK

Sport and Recreation

Bampton cricket, men versus ladies, in the 1950s. Ladies standing l-r: *Alice Taylor (umpire); Zena Taylor; Cathy Sowden; Mary Hulland; Rose Milton.* Kneeling: *Cathy Ford; Lily Pittey; Edna Edwards; Cathline Hutter; Betty Denner; Florence Hancock; Ann Collard.* RK

Bampton Rifle Club Trophy Winners, 1982. L-r: Tony Smith; Sarah Vincent; Bernard Lyons; Keith Batstone; Brian Seward. RK

Sport and Recreation

Bampton Scout Troop leaving the Church Institute for their annual camp in 1930. Standing l-r: Revd H.E. Frayling, Ern Serenger and Percy Hancock.

The first of 18 new cubs invested by Carol Stoyle and Group Scout Leader Brian Hookins, 1982. The cubs shown are Garry Totterdell, Bryan Hookins, Shaun Dale, John Morton, Bobby Hutter and Nicky Kennedy. RK

Bampton Girls Guildry and Boys Brigade, 1964. Front l-r: *Heather Castle, Susan Gardiner; Marion Coles; Hazel Munn; Mary Bellamy; Pamela Yendell.* Second row: *Pauline King; Shirley Mounce;* Third row: *Shirley Henderson; Jean Davey; Jill Hawkins; Denise Kingdon.* Fourth row: *Linda Yerberry; Jean Hawkins; Anne Kerslake; Vera Becks; Susan Herbert.* Boys Brigade l-r. *Toby Burnett; Michael Gardiner; Peter Wood; John Bellamy; Peter Bellamy; George Kingdon.* Second row: *Revd Howard Castle; David Moule; Tony Scott; David Yendell; Colin Smith; Robin Davey.* Back row: *Patrick Rendell; John Gardiner.* RK

Sport and Recreation

Judges and committee members at Bampton and District Horticultural Society Flower Show, 1979. RK

Bampton WI remains an essential part of the life of Bampton and much of the information included in this book comes from its members and records. These are members taken in 1982. L-r: Mrs Hockin; Mrs A. Bailey; Mrs Batt; Mrs M. Preece; Miss Pearson; Mrs C. Davey; Mrs E. Thomas (President); Mrs Reed; Mrs Bracken; Mrs L. Pittey. RK

Bampton Town Band playing at Bridgetown 1911.. Back row l-r: J. Herniman; J. Holland; J. Burnett; M. Jones; F. Burnett; J. Lazarus; H. Paul; J. Venn; T. Heal. Front row l-r: F. Lazarus; A, Paul; T. Davey; W, Bowden (Bandmaster); R. Kerslake; H. Sampson; J. Herniman jnr. RK

Bampton Town Band outside the vicarage, c.1950. Standing l-r: William Hancock; Ted Mutters; Michael Toze; Jack Venn; Jack Kelland; Alan Rowcliffe; Michael Rendell; Jack Herniman. Sitting l-r: Ern Gillard; Len Burnett; Cynthia Moore; Ned Northcott (Bandmaster); Margaret Gregory; Julia Gregory; Harry Sampson. Front: David Holland; Colin Webber. RK

Chapter 10 - Bampton Town Band

The earliest record of Bampton Town Band comes from a newspaper report in which it was recorded that Bampton Band was joined by Huntsham Band to play for a Mechanics Institution outdoor function in 1858. The first clear photograph we have is of our Band playing at Bridgetown in the Exe Valley in 1911.

In 1909, Bampton Town Band, according to the Women's Institute Bampton Scrapbook 1967-68. had only 14 members, but by 1958 these had grown to 30. It is likely that over the years numbers in the band have ebbed and flowed in this way, and the band may even have lapsed for a short while in its history.

The instruments were kept in a garage in Frog Street early this century. The uniforms were blue and gold, impressive to be seen, and worn with great pride.

The author was especially pleased to receive the 1942 photograph, lent by Joy Coles. Joy's father was bandmaster, Harry Sampson, and being taken in wartime, the photo shows all the bandsmen wearing their services uniforms, and look at those happy faces! The last Bandmaster was Mr Neddy Northcott, a jolly fellow, not very tall, but big-hearted with facial whiskers!. The band was his pride and joy as the beam on his face showed when leading them on parade.

The band had their own satirical set of Commandments:

1. Always make a point of being as late as possible for any rehearsal.. When you eventually arrive enter in a manner befitting your supreme importance. 2. In making your way through the band, endeavour to kick over as many stands as you can, the lads will love picking them up again. 3. When you are settled down (which should take a long time) take care that your instrument is not too nearly in tune with the others. It is always they that are wrong, not you. 4. If you haven't a part of the piece you are going to play, wait until the conductor is about to start before you tell anyone. 5. When the conductor is prepared to start you will take no notice. It is really the sign for everyone to start blowing and thumping as loudly as you can. 6. Should you by any chance make a wrong note, you should glare very hard at your nearest neighbour. He will enter into the spirit of the game and take all the blame. 7. Percussionists should always try and hit instruments, (especially symbols) or drop them in unexpected places so that it adds colour to chords. Of course it will not sound out of place. 8. Never take any notice of a little fellow in front waving a silly little stick about, he is only there for decoration and the Band must show him how it should go. 9. The music you play from is public property, so you can tear it and dog ear it as much as you like. There is a Librarian in the Band to look after it and he has a wonderful time repairing your damage with reams of sticky tapes. His only way of getting revenge is to cover up all the notes with thick brown paper. 10. When you finally pack up after an enjoyable rehearsal never give your music to the Librarian, let him chase all over the contryside for it, that is his job and he will love doing it.

The Band would not have encountered a more emotional time to play than for the last train at Bampton Station, on 5 October 1963. Bampton Town Band have always been in on the action including State celebrations, such as royal weddings, jubilee celebrations, and of course the end of the wars.

United Services Band, Bampton, October 1942. Back row l-r: *C. Cottrell; W. Rendell; R. Holland; J. Richards; L. Bowden; W. Gregory; J. Venn.* Front row: *E. Gillard; E. Northcott; W. Bowden; L. Burnett; H. Sampson; W. Hancock.* Photo Joy Coles

Territorial Volunteers and their mascot, prior to the Great War. Front right is Charlie Collard. Photo Clifford Lazarus

Chapter 11 - For King and Country

Wartime was traumatic for everyone. The men, some barely grown up, left the safety of their homes and loved ones knowing they may never see them again. For the families, especially the parents of the youngsters, there came fear for their offspring's life, or that of a husband or father.

However, we must not forget the women who through various jobs faced extreme danger. none more so than the nurses in field hospitals. Many perished as they strove to save the wounded.

Two World Wars have taken a toll on Bampton lives, yet on a brighter note some prisoners of war. who may otherwise never have found our town, were brought here. They married local girls and stayed, accepted in true Christian spirit as part of our community of Bampton.

Equally traumatised were thousands of young evacuees, torn for their own good away from their roots, and travelling many miles to a whole new way of life in the country. Many had never been close to an animal other than maybe a pet. There were fears and phobias to be won over, but probably it is fair to say country people are adaptable and ready to help others, especially children, in times of great crisis.

Many evacuees learnt to adapt very happily and still keep in touch with the friends made during the Second World War. One such lady wrote to the author when she heard about this book. Another lad, Ron MacDonald, who was nicknamed 'Bronco' lived at our bakery with my husband's family for years. Ron kept in touch from his new home in Tiverton until he recently passed away through ill health.

Some three hundred Bampton men served in the Armed Forces in the 1914–18 war. Many perished far from their homes, among them Anketell Moutray Read who was born at Castle Grove. Isabelle Kenny, who owns Castle Grove with her husband Ray, running it as a retirement home, wrote the following item for the book and enclosed the report regarding the death of Anketell:

In November 1915 a local newspaper brought pride to Bampton, Devon, with the following report:

'The Victoria Cross has been conferred on the late Captain Anketell Moutray Read, for an act of gallantry and devotion to duly. Captain Moutray Read was a son of Mrs Moutray Read who formerly resided at Little Breancamp, Washfield, and subsequently at Castle Grove, Bampton. Captain Moutray Read was a tall, smart, well-built officer, and frequently visited Bampton during his mother's stay at Castle Grove.'

The London Gazette *of 18 November 1915 records this citation for the award of the Victoria Cross:*

'For most conspicuous bravery during the first attack near Hulluch on the morning of 25 September 1915. Although partially gassed, Captain Rcad went out several times in order to rally parties of different units which were disorganised and retiring. He led them back into the firing line, and, utterly regardless of danger, moved freely about encouraging them under a withering fire. He was mortally wounded while carrying out this gallant work. Captain Read had previously shown conspicuous bravery during digging operations on 29th, 30th and 31st August 1915 and on the night of 29th-30th July he carried out of action an officer, who was mortally wounded, under a hot fire from rifles and grenades.'

Captain Read had previously served with the Royal Flying Corps and was renowned in the Army as an athlete and boxer who won the heavyweight boxing championship of India eight times and the middleweight twice. He also won the Army and Navy Heavyweight title thrice.

An old photograph shows the High Street – Luke Street road junction in 1900, or thereabouts. It is immediately noticeable that there is no war memorial. A second photograph, taken in the 1920s, we see the new war memorial commemmorating those men of Bampton who sacrificed their live in the Great War. There is also a window in the Parish Church with the names of local lives lost in this war.

Perhaps because of the threat of invasion, the

The view up High Street from Railway Bridge c. 1900. Compare this with the view below: there is no war memorial in place, although a telegraph (rather than telephone) pole can be seen jutting above the roofline of the shop. As always, the photographer has attracted a willing crowd of locals, eager to be part of the action. RK

Taken in the 1920s, this view shows the newly erected war memorial standing next to the finger post, absent form the earlier picture above, directing traffic to Dulverton and Minehead. A telephone post does little to enhance the scene. RK

The war memorial and floral tributes, taken in the 1930s. RK

Second World War, compared to the Great War, brought far more disruption to daily life in Bampton. Church bells were silenced and black-outs were adhered to, with force of law, if necessary. Local brothers, Tony and Geoff Chamberlain were young lads who thoughtfully extinguished the signal lights on the railway line, thinking they had been forgotten!

Men who were too old, or who were in reserved occupations, joined the Home Guard whose work is often humourously portrayed in programmes such as *Dad's Army*. Although we may laugh with relief that it was all a long time ago, the programme helps remind one how important the Home Guard was in reality.

Bampton also had a well-organised Royal Observer Corps that remained in force through-out the war, and thereafter. Eddy Crooks has been instumental in keeping interest for the young people in that Corps. They met regularly and sev-eral local residents over the years have enjoyed learning from all that the Corps could offer. It is only now, in 1998, that the Observer Post high on the Old Tiverton Road has been taken down.

Along with evacuees, the countryside was met with an invasion of Land Girls, women who joined the Land Army in order to offset the lack of labour caused through men going to war. These women performed all the tasks hitherto in the male domain, and life for them was often hard.

A 1998 film, *The Land Girls*, was made in Bampton and Dulverton, and follows the lives of these Land Army women. Several Bampton people appear in the film as extras.

The film uses Benshayes farm, home of Geoffrey and Tessa White (parents of Richard the present Lord Of The Manor of Bampton), on the edge of Bampton, as part of the location.

Lt-Cmdr Ninian Scott-Elliott lived in our town for ten years, where he became a familiar figure, seen dressed in a tweed safari-style jacket, doing his shopping. Few people realised he had a distin-guished war record until they read it in the news-paper after his death in 1998. He was awarded the Distinguished Service Cross for his actions in defending Malta during the Second World War.

He was one of 550 officers and men who went to Tobruk on a raid which turned out disastrous-ly, leading to their capture and impending impris-onment in Germany. As in many films featuring escapes from moving trains, this man actually did it! As the train sped him towards Germany Ninian escaped through the floor of the train and fled out across the Alps. Two more commands on destroyers followed before he retired from the forces and landed in 'Civvy Street'.

Lt-Cmdr Scott-Elliott always had a smile, making no secret that as bachelor he 'could not even boil an egg,' and that housekeeping was definitely not his favourite occupation. Asked 'How are you today,' his answer was always a quick and humourous 'Dying, twenty-four hours a day, I am practising dying.' Locals were used to this, and countered his quip by saying he was not doing very well at it!

Lt-Cmdr Scott-Elliott was 86 when he died in 1998. His one reported quotation was 'you will never get anywhere in this life if you only do what is wise!'

Edna May was evacuated to the Bampton area during the last war. Today, as Edna McNaughton, she recently visited Bampton and read about the plans for this book, offering the following contri-bution:

I was eleven years old, standing in the school at Shillingford, tired and hungry after a long train

For King and Country

Forget-me-not Day in Bampton, 28 October 1915. These women are selling posies which were sold in support of the men 'at the Front'. A poster reads 'Every Recruit Brings Peace Nearer'. Wendy Marchment's mother, Annie Atkins, is the girl in the light dress (no hat), her Aunt Lucy stands on Annie's right. RK

Bampton Home Guard, c.1940. Back row l-r: P. Penney; E. Gillard; D. Bowden; R. Smolden; Revd Jones (Baptist Minister); S. Salisbury; R, Milton; Jack Scott; Rundle. Fourth row: Tarr; R. Grabham; A. Woodman; V. Greenslade; G. Hutter; A. Hurford; A. Baker; W. Marley; J. Dunn; H. Tout; R. Baker; R. Mounce. Third row: H. Hancock; W. Walsh; F. Pook; R. Burnett; T. Peachey; A. Hutter; H. Caunter; F. Baker; H. Bowers; F. Parkman; L. Kelland; C. Cottrell. Second row: E. Balman; R. Burnett snr; L. Besley; H. Weston; A. Chudley; L. Gratton; F. Manley; L. Burnett; Dunn; G. Hill; W. Williams; L. Eckhart; T. Cottrell; Don Jones. Front row: G. Yeo; H. Taverner; F. Dunbar; G. Brewer; J. Hancock; S. Baker; H. Attwater; S. Coles; unknown; J. Fayter; P. Milton. RK

For King and Country

Above: *The Home Guard on Church Parade, marching down Luke Street, around 1944.* RK

Right: *Bampton men in uniform: Jack Coggins (left) and Fred Coles (father of Alan).* Photo June Coles

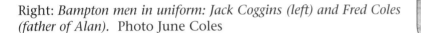

Bampton Home Guard Officers and NCOs, 1943. Back row l-r: *H. Weston; Ron Baker; Sam Hill; Tom Cottrell; Les Besley; L. Ekhart.* Middle row: *Len Gratton; Evan Collacott; Frank Manley; Col. Sir Gilbert Acland Troyte; Len Burnett; Col. Hockin; Jack Dunn; Albert Chudley.* Front row: *Rob Burnett; Ern Balman; Bill Williams; Donald Jones; Walt Randle.* RK

Bampton Home Guard, 1943.

journey from London, and wondering what was going to happen to me. My mother had seen me off on the coach outside my school, packed with my gas mask and lunch for the journey, and a few belongings. Some of my friends were left in the school with me, others having been dropped off at other destinations on the way. I was wondering where I was going to be billetted as there was a crowd of people in the school hall who were choosing the children they wanted to stay with them. I was one of the last to be picked, together with a

little girl called Rosina. We were both wearing wellington boots and were chosen by a farmer's wife, Mrs Ware, of Quartley Farm, Shillingford.

Some of the happiest times were spent during the eighteen months that I lived on the farm. I was well looked after and was amazed how much food there was, having lived on rationed food until then.

After school on my way home up the hill to Quartley I used to collect the cows from the field to take back for milking. I was scared when I first

Bampton County Secondary School, 1941, where, as a pupil Edna McNaughton shared her schooldays with Gerald Wensley, Leonard Arthurs, Raymond Rendell, Margaret Ware, Betty Tooze, Maud Bell, Gladys Henson, Henry Coggins, Gilbert Jones, Dennis Wensley, Wilfred Kelland, Peggy Summers, Bob Wakely, George Brice, Grace Buchanan, Bob Tanner, Austin Greenslade, Jimmy Lock, Les Woodman, Eileen Cottrell and Joan Thomas. Photo Edna MacNaughton

For King and Country

People of wartime Bampton. Clockwise from top: Dilwyn Cottrell, Reg Kingdon and Bernard Kingdon in uniform, 1945. The author's father, Frederick David Thomas, in Home Guard uniform c.1944. Photo author. Bampton AFC were strengthened by the inclusion of evacuee Ron 'Bronco' MacDonald (extreme right, front row). Others members of the same team are back row l-r: Bill Hartshorne; Joe Becks; Geoff Chamberlain; Len Mounce; Cliff Baker; Les Knight (policeman); Jack Herbert (trainer). Front: Alan Baker; Howard Pershouse; Cliff Fowler; Alec Hancock. The pitch was at Shillingford Road. L/Cpl Reg Kingdon in the Gordon Highlanders, 51st Highland Division, 1945. RK

Filming The Land Girls, *1998. Alan Rowland, fourth from left.* Photo A. Roland

Bampton children dressed for parts as extras in The Land Girls. *Back row l-r: Sam Wheeler; Michael Vile; Carl Burton; Ryan Payne; Andrew Westacott; Peter Davis; David Woolacott; Susan Roberts (teacher); David McKee; Kim Burnett; Sam Cottrell. Front: Kyle Stanley; Toby Oakley; Mark Shere; Ned Parker; Richard Ayre; Rupert Harvey; Tim Lewis; Henry Oakley.* Photo B. Burnett

used to do this, not having been in close contact with cows before, but I soon got used to it and enjoyed it.

After milking, the churns used to be left in the dairy with cold water running on them and the next day they had thick cream on top of the milk. This was really delicious and I had many tastings. Mrs Ware also made wonderful clotted cream, that was readily eaten with scones or bread and jam, and I have loved it ever since.

There used to be a granary opposite the farm-house and I would go in there and run my hands throught the corn and bran and animal feed. One day, while Mr Ware was having a conversation with somone, I went to the top of the granary steps and climbed on a horse that was standing there and started walking downhill with it. I was chastised in no uncertain terms and did not attempt to do anything like it again!

Some of my other memories are the haymaking and harvesting in the fields. We used to put corn into 'stooks' ready for when the thresher came, and people came from different farms to help. We used to take the baskets of food and cold tea and cider for the workers' lunch, which was thoroughly enjoyed. This was a very happy time for me. Coming from London I had no experince of country life. Another memory was making cider in the cider press in outhouse. The apples were pressed between layers of straw and the juice squeezed out by turning the screw and compressing the layers. I remember how sweet the first juice was.

I used to attend the little Chapel in Shillingford on Sundays for Sunday School. I did win a prize there (a book), I think we had to collect so many texts (small pictures with a Bible Reading on them).

The village shop was my stopping place on my way home from school when I would spend my pocket money on sweets or a comic. I was at school in Shillingford, until moving to school in Bampton. I used to miss the bus home if we were late leaving school, then I had to walk miles home to Quartley. Once, when walking home with friends, one dashed across the road to pick some primroses on the bank and she was knocked down by a car. We were all very frightened and remember she was away from school a long time. She was unlucky as there were not many cars in 1941!

After I had been at Quartley for some time my mother and brother came to stay on the next farm, which was West Holcombe, non-existent now, with Dorothy and Robert Ellicott. This led to many happy times for the family, and my mother and father kept in touch with them all through the years. They spent many happy holidays there and we do the same, still enjoying our visits to Shillingford and Bampton, able to reminisce of times past. Some places do not change a lot and Devon is still glorious!

Top: *Students and teachers of the Devon County Dairy School, outside the Drill Hall, 1895. These touring schools gave lessons and exhibitions encouraging modern practices in dairying.* Above: *Celebrating the winning of the Cox Cup in the Best Large Village Section of Britain in Bloom, 1996. Bampton has competed for almost thirty years and has achieved consistent success thanks to the hard work and commitment of the people of Bampton. In 1998 Bampton was the only West Country entry to gain a national title.* BS

Chapter 12 - A Bampton Miscellany

There is so much to be said and written About Bampton. Almost a thousand photographs, newspaper cuttings and other artefacts have been provided for possible use in this book and it is impossible to include it all in one book. These final few pages include a mixture of pictures of people, places and events that reflect the diversity of our wonderful town.

Celebrating 50 years of the Town Council in April 1985. L-r: Phyllis Marley, Norman Cleverly; Edward Tanner; Shirley Banbury; Rex Serenger; Reg Kingdon; Frank Batt; Doreen Shore; David Smith; Diana Thomas. RK

Above left: Twinning, Unveiling the name plaque Rue de Bampton in Villers Bocage, Normandy, 1978. Above right: Protesters make their views known over planning enquiry into the use of Higher Kiln as a tipping site in 1979. The objectors lost the initial battle but later got the tip closed. RK

Being on the edge of Exmoor means that Bampton has had its fair share of bad weather over the years and in earlier days was subject to annual floods.

Above: *Floods at New Buildings in the 1950s.* RK

Left: *Ted Mantle's Dairy flooded in the early 1900s.* Photo Sally Luxton

Below: *Snow in the harsh winter of 1963.* Photo Dorothy Ellicott

Right: *Bampton's first charabanc, The Stag, 1910.* RK

Below: *Father Christmas visits Bampton by train, 1950.* Photo K. Burnett

Right: *Sophie Burston and Brendan Tayler in their 1949 carnival entry 'Darby and Joan'. They won first prize.* RK

Today Rex Serenger supplies the motorist, and others, with their everyday needs. BS

Although this book can contain only a small fragment of what is Bampton's history, the photographs and the people in them show us that, although times change, communities remain essentially the same - it is people that make places what they are.

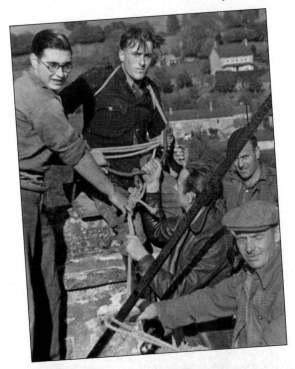

Top left: *Les Woodman (at it again - he's like a cat and must have nine lives). Here, in 1947, he's about to go over the edge of the church tower to remove a tree growing next to the clock. L-r: Rex Serenger, Les Woodman, Ern Serenger, Charlie Sowden, George Shard.* Top right: *Alan Hutter, who once bulldozed his own house in order to remove a tenant who refused to leave.* Above: *It could be you! The author, her husband Brian, Karen Hussey, and son Roger, display the National Lottery promotional poster in their shop.*

THE NEXT GENERATION

Bampton pre-school group, 1998. 1. Jean Pope; 2. Karen Walter; 3. Mandy Payne; 4. Ben Gutteridge; 5. Kieron Hole; 6. Joseph Clarke; 7. Robert Walter; 8. Joe Shutler; 9. Adam Shore; 10. Flynn McManus; 11. Luke Strong; 12. Tyler Smith; 13. Ashleigh Smith; 14. Alison Coles; 15. James Philp; 16. Jennifer Atkinson; 17. Emma Rayfield. BS

Reg and Joyce Kingdon.

Reg Kingdon

Who is this Reg Kingdon? This is a question a few people reading this book may ask. To almost everyone else in Bampton and a wide surrounding area Reg is known as the Bampton Historian. What was originally a personal interest became a fascinating hobby as Reg compiled a huge collection of photographs of Bampton's past. Coupled to this he kept all current information about Bampton and its people mostly in newspaper clippings, and as time went on Reg needed more and more room for his files.

Thus, where Donald Gould (who helped so much with the Scotts Quarries section) has a great wealth of knowledge about Bampton, Reg has supporting visual information.

Local people who turned out old photographs when spring cleaning offered them to Reg to add to his swelling collection. Many of these he transferred on to slides so that he could give slide shows locally. They were a big hit as locals recognised familiar faces and saw how their town looked long ago. Nowadays the author's husband, Brian, takes care of the slide collection. Hundreds upon hundreds of bits and pieces record the good, the bad, and often the funny side of long and not so long ago. 'It really is a labour of love,' Reg told me as he showed me file after file, so proudly.'

Today Reg can be seen walking near his home, Leburn House, in Luke Street. Reckoned to be one of the oldest buildings in Bampton, along with Town Mill (Manor Mill) and the Swan Hotel.

Joyce, Reg's patient wife, has got used to Reg popping out for 'a few moments', returning a couple of hours later. The penalty for being so well known!

Reg has led an active life through playing sport and being a councillor, along with his regular job. He worked at Seward's when he left school, aged 14, and says that it was the best job he ever had because he was constantly talking to local people and sharing their lives.

Reg was born at Petton and married local girl, Joyce. They have two daughters, Denise, the hairdresser in Newton Square, and Paula, who has worked ever since leaving school with the author,

in the shop, and for many years on the bread rounds. That was great fun (and hard work) in all winds and weathers, and involved such activities as digging the van out of snow drifts. Vernon is the baby of the family and runs his own building business in Bampton.

A tall once slimline figure, Reg was suitably athletic, becoming a PT instructor in the army. He loves cricket and football and represented the services in both. He took part in the D-Day landings and served over five years in the army. Wounded in Normandy, Reg returned home. He remembers those locals who did not come home at the Service of Remembrance each year at our War Memorial. For many years as Chairman of the town council, Reg laid the wreath for his fellow men.

While Reg was paid five shillings at first in Seward's, this rose eventually to seventeen shilling and sixpence. (During that time he even managed to fall through the bakehouse roof!). When he 'joined up' his pay dropped to 1O/6d.

A job that took Reg to Massachusetts in the USA was with Heathcoats Factory in Tiverton. In America Reg learned the scientific knowledge in making rubber core thread. While in Fall River Reg was honoured with the Key To The City of Fall River.

Bampton AFC have fifty years of support from Reg to look back on, he was player, committee member, chairman and always, as now, a great supporter. In return the club made him Hon. Life Vice President.

Reg and Joyce live in what may have originally been the vicarage as their back door leads into the churchyard. Having been a sidesman, bellringer, chorister and churchwarden during fifty years, he was made Warden Emeritus for his life long service. Another Emeritus award was from the Royal British Legion for 30 years service.

Reg was in at the beginning of the Britain in Bloom competiton in Bampton and has been chairman of the Bampton Over 60s Club, started by his former employer, Arnold Seward. This books is dedicated to Reg and to the people he has served so well over the years.

Subscribers

Mervyn and Jean Adams, Morebath, Devon

Gordon And Ida Alderman, Bristol

Edith Alderman

Derek and Marg Aldridge, Bampton, Devon

Gail and Peter Alford, Willand, Devon

Anglo International Group, Bampton, Devon

Gillie and Robert Appleby, Bampton, Devon

Mrs M. Ashdown, Bampton, Devon

Mr and Mrs A. Attwater, Bampton, Devon

Mr Ayres, Bampton, Devon

Mrs E.F. Bailey, Bampton, Devon

Alan Eric Baker, Cove, Tiverton, Devon

Annette and Martyn Baker, Rill House, Shillingford, Devon

Penny and Nigel Baker, Bampton, Devon

Wilf and Margaret Baker, Shillingford, Devon

Dr Anthony S. Baker, Bampton, Devon

Mr William S. Baker, Bampton, Devon

Mr E.W.G. Balman, Bampton, Devon

Bampton Family, Australia

Bampton Society, Bampton, Devon

Bampton/Villers Bocage Twinning Association

Arthur and Shirley Banbury, Bampton, Devon

P.J. and P.M. Barthram, Bampton, Devon

Flora and Christopher Bartlett, Petton, nr Bampton, Devon

Robin Barwell, Stoodleigh, Devon

G. and V. Bayliss, Bampton, Devon

Andrew and Naomi Beal, Shillingford, Devon

Mike, Kelly, Charlotte, Joshua and Timothy Beeston, Morebath, Devon

Ann E. Bennett, Bampton, Devon

David and Jenny, Berks

Dorothy Binding, Watchet, Somerset

Esmee and Kenneth W. Blackwell, Bampton, Devon

Doreen and Derek Bolt

Wendy Boothroyd and Brian Hughes, Bampton, Devon

Mrs D.C. Brammer, Shillingford, Devon

Gerald C. Breeze, previously of Bampton, Devon

Len, Alec and Freda Brewer, Bampton, Devon

John Broom, Bampton, Devon

Mrs Anne Broom, Burnham on Sea

Tess Burgess, Bampton, Devon

R.M. and D. Burnell, Old Mill Guest House, Shillingford, Devon

Mrs B. Burnett, Bampton, Devon

Mrs K.M. Burnett, Bampton, Devon

Mrs Winifred V.B. Burnett, Tiverton, Devon

Nigel S. Carter, Hereford

Joan and Geoff Chamberlain, Bampton, Devon

Mr and Mrs N. Chanan, Bampton, Devon

John and Gillian Chanter, Bampton, Devon

Mrs Paula R.S. Charles, Yeo Mill, Devon

Gerald B.D. Chidwick, Bampton, Devon

John M. Christie, Bampton, Devon

Caroline Christie, Manali, India

Mike Clark, Bampton, Devon

Mary and Norman Claydon, Bampton, Devon

Keith M. Cleeve, Tiverton, Devon

Joyce Cleeve, Bampton, Devon

Norman Cleverley, Bampton, Devon

Brenda and Edwin Cliffin, Bampton, Devon

Mrs C. Cobb, South Wigston, Leicester

Sue and Stuart Coles, Tiverton, Devon

D.D. Coles, Bampton, Devon

June and Alan Coles, Shillingford, Devon

Cliff and Barbara Coles, Bampton, Devon

Bill and Joyce Coles, Australia

T.J. Coles, Tiverton, Devon

Simon P. Coles, Bampton, Devon

Alan and Ann, Collard, Bampton, Devon

Mr R.A. Collard, Worksop, Notts.

Elizabeth Colvile (née White), Dulverton, Somerset.

Coney Family, Bampton, Devon

Cooke Family (née Venner), Bampton, Devon

Eric Cottrell, Bampton, Devon

Mrs S.M. Courtney, Bampton, Devon

Mrs Kay Crandall, San Diego, California, U.S.A.

Eddie And Vida Crooks, Bampton, Devon

Mrs Janet Cross, Huntsham, Devon

E.E. Crouch, Bampton, Devon

Cis Croucher, Bampton, Devon

Peter Cruttwell, Windwhistle, Bampton, Devon

C.S. Cullen, Tucking Mill Farm, Bampton, Devon

Mrs E.J. Curling (Betty Oxenham), Southampton

Veronica and Norman Curran, Bampton, Devon

Mr and Mrs B.M. Currie, Bampton, Devon

Raymond Curtis, Bamptonian (born 1932)

David Dagge, Bampton, Devon

Mr H. Dart, Tiverton, Devon

John and Mary, Davey, Tiverton, Devon

Jon C. Davey, Claygate, Surrey

Richard B. Davey, Bampton, Devon

Drs J. and M. Davies, Bampton, Devon

Godfrey and Sally Davis, Skilgate, Taunton, Somerset

Mrs Joan Day, Bampton, Devon

Susan de Mey, Bampton, Devon

Charlotte and Christopher de Vere Moss, Horfield, Bristol

Denner Family

Penny and Raymond Dennis, Petton, Nr Bampton, Devon

William Dennis, Petton, Nr Bampton, Devon

A.W. Dixson, Bishops Lydeard, Somerset

Julia Donnelly, Bampton, Devon

Jean Doyle (née Hancock), Exeter

Brian and Pam Dunesby, Bampton, Devon

John Dunn, Bampton, Devon

Prudence Edwards, Cheltenham

Paul Edworthy, Bradninch, Devon

Dorothy L. Ellicott, Petton, Devon

Prof. Raymond A. Elliott, Bow, Crediton, Devon

Mrs Dianne Evans, Ontario, Canada

Bertie Evans, Shillingford, Devon

Henry and Elsie Farrow, Shillingford, Devon

Andrew Fay, Bookham, Surrey

Vincent Fay, Bampton Joinery, Bampton, Devon

John G. Fayter, Tiverton, Devon

Elizabeth M. Ferris, née Evans, Mylor, Cornwall

George Floyd, Shillingford, Devon

Mr J.N. Fordham, Bampton, Devon

Dean and Faye Fowler-McDowell, Bampton, Devon

Mrs B. Froud, Wiveliscombe, Somerset

Mr T. Gannon, Bampton, Devon

Eddie and Zena Gannon, Taunton, Somerset

Michael Gannon, Kings Lynn, Norfolk

Olive Gardner (née Alderman), Weston-Super-Mare

Mrs Gaventa, Shillingford

Dilwyn R. Gibbins, Tiverton, Devon

Maureen E. Gibbs, Nomansland, Tiverton, Devon

Anita M. Gooding, Morebath, Devon

Dorothy Goodwin, Derbyshire

Elaine and Jim Goodwin, Bampton, Devon

Donald Gould (formerly of Bampton), York

Mrs J. Gratton, Bampton, Devon

Lord Ambrose and Lady Rosalynne Greenway, Morebath, Devon

F.L. Griffiths, West Yelland, Barnstaple, Devon

Julia E.M. Gullidge, Bampton, Devon

William E. and Olive C. Hampton, Bampton, Devon

Alec J. Hancock, Exeter, Devon

Linda Hancock, Huntsham, Devon

Ivy J. Hancock

Ray Harris, Halberton, Tiverton, Devon

Moira and Tony Harrowell, Bampton, Devon

Susan Hartshorne, Bampton, Devon

Maureen Hartshorne, Bampton, Devon

Mr M. and Mrs P. Hatchett, Bampton, Devon

Mr Kenneth H. Hawkins, Tiverton, Devon

Eileen and Michael Hawkins, Bampton, Devon

Mary E. Hawkins (née Harvey), previously of Brook Street, Bampton

Nicky Hayes, Bampton, Devon

Jon D. Healy, Three Bridges, Sussex

D.T. Heard, Tiverton, Devon

M. Hellings, Reigate, Surrey

Jonathon Hill, Bampton and Exeter, Devon

Mrs Sheila Hill, Clayhanger, Devon

Richard J. Hiscocks MA, Oakfordbridge, Bampton, Devon

Mr P. Holland, Tiverton, Devon

Albert Edward Hookins, Bampton, Devon

Mrs P. Hookins, Bampton, Devon

Anne-Marie Hourigan, Bampton, Devon

L.M. Hubbard, Bampton, Devon

Val and Jerry Hughes, Shillingford, Devon

Alison Hulls, Cranwell

Susi Hunt, previously of Ivy Cottage, Bampton

Fred and Iris Hutchings, Bampton, Devon

Mrs Margaret Hutchings, Bampton, Devon

Colin R. Hutter, Bampton, Devon

Mr R.M. Hutter, Tiverton, Devon

Jennifer R. Hutter, Millhead, Bampton, Devon

Alan R. Hutter, Shillingford, Devon

Greta Isaac (née Lazarus), Chevithorne, Devon

Sylvia Jansen, Canterbury, Kent

Mrs J.F. Jenkins, Bampton, Devon

The Rev. and Mrs I.L. Johnson, Manchester

Mrs Diana Jones, Salt Spring Island, Vancouver, BC.

Mrs Doreen Jones, Bampton, Devon

Wendy King, Bampton, Devon

Shirley Kingdon, Bampton, Devon

Mr John P. Knowles, Stoodleigh Barton, Devon

A.E. Law, Bampton, Devon

Mr C. Lazarus, Shillingford, Devon

Hilda and Susan Leach, Bampton, Devon

Fred and Ann Leach, Bampton, Devon

Jonathan and Debbie Leach, Exeter, Devon

Vera Lees, née Kingdon, Birmingham, West Midlands

Richard Lethbridge, Chittlehamholt, Devon

A.J. Lewis, Tiverton, Devon

Clare Lloyd, Bampton, Devon

Loftus Family, Bampton, Devon

John and Sally, Luxton, Petton, Nr Bampton, Devon

Mark, Denise, Danielle and Luke Lyons, Bampton, Devon

Sarah and Philip Malpass, Bampton, Devon

Wendy Marchment, Hants (daughter of Annie Atkins)

Edric and Daphne Markland, New Romney, Kent

Raymond J. Marley, Bampton, Devon

William I. Marshall, Stafford, Staffs

Graham Neville Matthews (formerly of Bampton), Boston, U.S.A.

Mrs Anne Mclean Williams (née Bullen), Bampton, Devon

Tom McManamon, Tiverton, Devon

Edna D. McNaughton, Harlow, Essex

Adrian Mills, Morebath, Devon

Mr Kenneth P.F. Milton, Taunton, Somerset

Mrs A. Milton, Bampton, Devon

David Moore, Brockenhurst, Hampshire (Bampton A.F.C. - mid 1950s)

Derek and Gillian Mounce, Bampton, Devon

Michael G. Mutter, former Headboy 1955-1957

John and Anne Nevill, Bampton, Devon

W.A. Osborne, Bampton, Devon

Mr and Mrs G. Page, Hockworthy, Somerset

June and Dennis Palfrey, Morebath, Devon

Amanda and Ian Parker, Clyst St Mary, Devon

Mrs M. Parkman, Tiverton, Devon

Nigel A. Payne, Shillingford, Devon

Mr Pearson, Bampton, Devon

Sylvia and Esme Pearson, Bampton, Devon

Liz and Danny Penney, Bampton, Devon

Mr David J. Phillips, Bampton Primary School, Bampton, Devon

Mr W.J. Phillips and Mrs S.E. Miller, Bampton, Devon

Mike and Wendy Powell, Bampton, Devon

J. E. and R. Proietti, Bampton

David Pugsley, Cullompton, Devon

Don and Sylvia Pulsford, Uffculme, Devon

Christine and Stuart Pulsford, Bampton, Devon

Lynne Rawlinson (née Crooks), Plympton, Devon

Mrs S.E. Record, Bampton, Devon

Mrs Sue Reece, Silver Brook Salon, Bampton, Devon

Gordon W. and Peggy I. Reed, Morebath, Devon

Hedley and Jenni Rees, Bampton, Devon

Peter and Cindy Riley, Bampton, Devon

A.J. Rooks, Tiverton, Devon

Kenneth A. Rose, Skilgate, Taunton, Somerset

Alan and Sheila Rowland, Bampton, Devon

Janet and John Rudd, Bampton, Devon

Sophie Russell, Bampton, Devon

David Russell, Mickleover, Derby

Diego and Corine Saldana, Albertville, France

Ian, Essie, Tony and Steve Scott, Burnham-on-Sea, Somerset.

Diane E. Seary (née Vernon), Bampton Police Station - 1960s

Mr P.R.E. Serenger, Bampton, Devon

Richard and Dee Seward, Northampton

Dorothy L. Seward, Bampton, Devon

Roger and Dawn Seward, Bampton, Devon

Ms P. Sheppard (née Ware), Bournemouth, Dorset

John and Angela Slade, Bampton, Devon

Mr R.C. Sloman, Bampton, Devon

Margaret and Jim Smale, Northam, Devon

Jenny and David Smith, Huntsham, Devon

Alan L. Smith, Bampton, Devon

Sylvia and Graham Smith, Leamington Spa

P.A. Soper, Bampton, Devon

John Sowden, Bampton, Devon

Diana Stewart, Carrickfergus, Scotland

Gerald and Ann Stoneman, Tiverton, Devon

Robert and Helen Stoneman, Uffculme, Devon

Ray, Jill, Martyn and Jason Stoneman, Bampton, Devon

R. and A. Stoneman, Swimbridge, Devon

Chris and Carol Stoyle, Bampton, Devon

Mr and Mrs A.W .Strachan, Dowhills, Bampton, Devon

Roy Strong, Bampton, Devon

Mrs C. Stuart, Godalming, Surrey

Clive and Nina Summerfield, Northampton

Christine Swain (née Milton), Hayes, Middlesex

Jean Swanston (née Burnett), Wiveliscombe, Somerset

C.N. Sworder, Oakford, Devon

Edward and Pauline Tanner, Bampton, Devon

Clifford G. and Margaret M. Tarr, Blackpool, Lancs

Alan and Val Taylor, Carriage Way House, Bampton, Devon

Mr Raymond V. Taylor, Tiverton, Devon

Brian, Paula, Debbie and Andrew Thomas, Bampton, Devon

Mrs S. J. Thompson, Bampton, Devon

William, John, Michael, and Jacky Totterdale, Bampton, Devon

Jacqueline A. Tovey, Wonham Kiln, Bampton, Devon

Tony and Ann Trigg, Bampton, Devon

Michael Truelove, Bampton, Devon

Arthur Tucker, Bampton, Devon

Natasha M. Van Riel, Bampton, Devon

Jim and Mabel Vellacott, Bampton, Devon

Brian Vodden, Exeter, Devon

David Vodden, Tiverton, Devon

Marjorie Vodden, Bampton, Devon

Mr and Mrs Waite, Bampton, Devon

Mr Tony Waite, Tiverton, Devon

C.P. Ware, Kent

F.T. Ware, Cove, Devon

Mike and Anthea Waters, Bampton, Devon

Julia Watson (née Powell), Grantham, Lincs.

Keith J. Webber, Sandford, Bristol

Colin, Stella, Julie and Jane Webber, Bampton, Devon

Josephine M. Wensley, Bampton, Devon

Geoff and Tessa White, Bampton, Devon

Mr and Mrs White, Bampton, Devon

Simon and Annette Williams, Morebath, Devon

Jill and Tony Williams, Bampton, Devon

Roy Wilson, Bampton, Devon

Michael Witcher, Winterslow, Salisbury, Wilts

Tim Witcher, Herts (grandson of Annie Atkins)

Mr Peter W. Wood, Bampton, Devon

Mrs V. Wood, Tiverton, Devon

Robert J. Woodman, Washfield, Tiverton, Devon

Leslie A. Woodman, Bampton, Devon

Rosemary Woodward, Maidstone, Kent

J.C. Yandle, Barnes, London, SW13

Willie Yendell, West Draton, Middlesex

V. Yeo, Bridgwater, Somerset

Marcia Yeo Cleverley